BORN TO REWILD

Triumphs from a Now Fearless Woman

Manda Kalimian

Born To Rewild

This is a smart book which means whenever you see a QR code you can scan it with your smart phone and visit the linked content. For example, scan the code below to visit the image gallery for the book or visit www.borntorewild.com/gallery

Exclusive Distributors: APG
ISBN: 9781953652881 (Hardback)
Library of Congress Control Number: 2021933822
1st Edition
This book, story, and any associated content is protected. © Copyright 2021 by Manda Kalimian.
Published by Imagine and Wonder Publishers, New York. 28 Sycamore Lane, Irvington New York, NY10533
United States of America. Telephone: 646.644.0403

Story by Manda Kalimian.
Writing by Darley Newman.
Scientific oversight and additional writing by Dr. Ross D. MacPhee
Design, writing, editing, and direction by Dr. Simon E. Mills.

DEDICATION

To America's wild horses on who's backs this country was built, wars were won, and heroes were made. We are forever in your debt.

To you, the wild at heart, kept in cages; may you find your wings.

OUR JOURNEY

PREFACE

We live in a time of crushing change and unrest. The world is at a turning point, and we with it. Our individual lives and journeys are all interconnected. It is a moment in time to stop and listen to the voices within ourselves and what they are saying about our individual roles at this time. What can we do to ensure the health of our planet and civilization, as we know it? What will we teach our children, who will they be, and what are we leaving them?

When something so powerful and important resonates within, it is our responsibility as humans to follow that voice and calling. This is one such story.

My love and passion for our wild horses have led me on a journey of self-empowerment, realization, and rewilding. It is through this journey that I am learning who I <u>am</u> and who I can be. This journey awaits us all if we choose to open our hearts to hear our innate reason and who we want to be while discovering who we really are.

I hope that by sharing my journey with you that you will be open to seeing your calling. There are no rules, and there are no prerequisites to finding your path. You just have to ask to be shown; that is your first step.

So, join me on my rewilding journey to save our wild horses. It's been a crazy ride, and it's not over!

As you read these pages, you will see that I refer repeatedly to America's indigenous people. Many views exist on the correct terminology, and not wishing to offend anybody; I want to clarify why, at times, I use American Indian in this context. One of the principal characters on this journey whom you are about to meet, Moses Brings Plenty, A Lakota Sioux, calls himself an Indian and considers 'American' redundant. American is inferred. Others find this term offensive and prefer Native American. Whatever your view, when I refer to the original inhabitants of this land, I only do so with the deepest respect.

1. REWILDING

Minutes away from rescuing a team of wild horses that I had promised freedom to, I thought I was ready—believing that when these horses were set free, I would miraculously feel the same freedom in my heart and soul. But Mo had some bad news to share with me.

"Manda, Prairie sent me a text and said not to come with the horses today," he stated, matter-of-factly.

I cocked my head sideways, sure that I didn't hear him correctly.

"What! What do you mean not to come?" I could feel the blood leave my face, my knees buckling under me.

Mo, reading a text message aloud, "I have a problem. My dad said my aunt wants to fight me for my land, saying part of it is hers. The Bureau of Indian Affairs (BIA) says I can't use the land now. They're saying I don't own all the land. It doesn't belong to me. They want to lease it out. Don't come today."

My mouth fell open as I entered his musty hotel room. I didn't even know where to start.

"Her aunt went to the judge—she's jealous because all of the land went to Prairie instead of her. The aunt's got some kind of 'in' with the judge, and even though it's not legal, they're telling Prairie the land isn't hers," Mo explained.

It sounded like an episode of The Jerry Springer Show.

"Okay." My heart was beating fast, and I felt a little dizzy. I didn't know how to reply or even what to ask next.

"Her aunt says if she even sees horses on the land, she'll shoot them," Mo said. I stopped by one of the beds, frozen by his words and mesmerized while I watched him methodically braid his long hair into two braids. He'd finally decided that the first braid was satisfactory. He was starting the other as he leaned against the room's air conditioning unit. Mo, a Lakota Sioux, was meticulously neat with long braids that extend down past his hips, but today, his unkempt appearance was giving me even more anxiety.

"Prairie's driving into the court in Rapid City now to see what she can do."

"Thanks, MO. I can't believe this! Is it not her land? Who can I call and what can I do?"

I stumbled over to the desk, grabbed its edge with my left hand to steady myself, and caught my breath. I used my right to frantically search through my phone, hoping one of my contacts would spark an idea. I wondered if Senator Chuck Schumer's office could help or who I knew in politics right now that could put things right. I was sure it was useless. I was dealing with Indian country where their own legal system reigned supreme.

"Land rights are pretty tricky for us," Mo explained. "Reservation land is held 'in trust' for us by the federal government. It's owned and managed by the Bureau of Indian Affairs, which is totally corrupt. Keeping control of the land keeps the people down because we can't utilize it. If you have control of your land, you can farm, you can lease it, you can do whatever you want. The BIA leases out the land. They give you the money, but the money is on the dollar. They keep the hedge."

"What does that mean?" my voice rose in volume and octaves.

At that very moment, Mo got a call back from Prairie.

"P- put her on speaker," I commanded while stuttering.

Mo nodded. The connection was horrible. Prairie's voice kept cutting in and out.

"I'm driving to Rapid City courthouse to see if I can get an order from the judge," she said in intermittent bursts.

I was already googling the driving distance from Prairie's house to the Rapid City Courthouse.

"Do you think you'll be able to resolve this today," I whispered as loudly as I could without talking. I was wound up tight, and my desperation was high.

"What?" the line crackled and hissed. "Not far, but I..." And then we lost the signal.

It was a three-and-a-half-hour drive from Prairie's land to Rapid City, but I didn't even know if she'd just left her driveway or was almost there. Who the heck knew if what she was saying was even true!

Oh my god, what was I going to do now, I thought to myself. I sat there for a good long minute before I looked up at myself in the mirror. How did I get here? What was I thinking? Why would I think I could even pull something like this off? I looked back down at my well-worn paddock boots. I couldn't even look at those. A wave of shame crept from my stomach to my throat, and I swallowed hard. I'd been working for over a decade to get here, running a non-profit through all the struggles, hurdles, and successes that come along with small business life. As a lifelong horsewoman, I thought I was ready. I should have known it was too good to be true back in October.

It was October of 2016 when we had a lead on a property. I remember the date well, as it was the time of the protests at Standing Rock. I was working with Mo and Jon on a music video, part of which we filmed in New York City in Times Square and partly out West in North Dakota. We wanted to create a song to inspire awareness of the plight of American Indians and wild horses.

Thousands of protesters gathered in Cannon Ball, North Dakota, on a site slated to be dug up to run a controversial oil pipeline, the Dakota Access Pipeline. It would funnel over a half a million barrels of crude oil each day from North Dakota to Illinois. It also ran the risk of contaminating the Missouri River and thus the water supply for the Standing Rock Sioux, a tribe of around 10,000 whose reservation in the central part of North and South Dakota is the sixth largest in the United States.

The project had already disrupted burial sites sacred to the Sioux. As more protestors gathered, including lots of young people, the news media started to take notice. The team at my foundation, the Cana Foundation, had as well. We decided to go out and film the protests so we could include this important piece of history in our video but also to stand behind the Sioux. Moses Brings Plenty, one of our team members at Cana and an advocate for wild horses, is Lakota Sioux. He's a direct descendant of Brings Plenty, an Oglala Lakota warrior who fought in the Battle of Little Big Horn.

As the founder of Cana and a passionate advocate of American Indian and wild horse rights, I was determined to go to Standing Rock to help with the filming and simply be there to experience the protests, but it was a holiday, and my husband Albert insisted that I be with the family. It wasn't worth getting into a fight with Albert over something related to my work again. It killed me that I couldn't be there myself, but I was glued to my phone and email, receiving regular dispatches from Mo and Dana, my Long Island assistant who I had sent on my behalf.

Mo was reporting back updates saying that the situation there was becoming intense. For our work with Cana, he'd spoken with a woman named Ladonna Brave Bull, a Sioux tribe historian, and an activist. Along with Phyllis Young and Pearl Means, Ladonna was one of the main women leading the charge.

Our goal in visiting the protests was two-fold—capture footage for our campaign and connect with people who might have land and be willing to take in wild horses. Our organization was working to help get wild horses out of the holding pens in which tens of thousands were being held by one of our government organizations, the Bureau of Land Management. The BLM was rounding up horses and taking them off their rightful lands to favor cattle ranchers and special interest groups who want to drill and frack.

Our goal was to ideally place these wild horses on American Indian lands, the lands that were originally their home. Reconnecting these wild horses with native communities was a natural fit for helping to restore the environment while helping indigenous communities to reconnect to the spirituality of the horse—and, in turn, their self-empowerment. These efforts were part of larger rewilding initiatives to help the environment go back to a previous, more natural state.

Ladonna introduced Mo to her daughter, Prairie. Prairie had about 5,000 acres near Standing Rock, and Ladonna said she might be willing to take some horses.

"I spoke with Prairie," Mo said over the phone. "She wants to take a couple of hundred horses."

"That's unbelievable," I said, nearly jumping up and down in the hallway of my Long Island stables. "We have to see the land. Find out if there's running water, if it's fenced..."

I reeled through a list of thoughts and questions as I marched into my office, ready to try and find satellite imagery of Prairie's land. I wanted to act fast so as not to lose this opportunity. This could be the lead I needed to finally accomplish my goal of releasing wild horses on native lands. It wasn't only a dream. It was my purpose and my job to change the fate and destiny of these wild horses and our environment.

My plan was to adopt as many horses as I could from the BLM to get them out of the holding pens where they were living these trapped and unnatural lives and rewild them; set them free. Our foundation would handle the adoption process, and someone like Prairie would then host the horses on her land. Our foundation would then help the locals to create healing and teaching programs for the community around these wild horses that were now working to revitalize the lands.

Adopting a wild horse is a big deal for anyone, but especially for me, with a publicly facing foundation with alliances with politicians and celebrities. It was my lifelong goal to rewild horses and lands, but I was still not one to rush into this without thinking through the details—even though I'd already waited over a decade. There was always something new to consider on all fronts.

Through my connections with Steve Israel, a New York State Congressman, I'd been introduced to some BLM higher-ups. I knew about the general adoption process, but it got a bit more stringent when one asked for dozens of horses. Steve advised me on the do's and don'ts.

"Never ask the BLM to pay for the shipping," Steve told me on a visit to my Long Island farm, as he walked my horse Rusty around the meadow. Steve had visited my farm a few times and grown quite close to Rusty. "Make it as easy as you can for them to say yes and want to work with you."

He gave Rusty a pat on the neck and stroked his white nose. A chestnut colored horse, Rusty was one of our show horses and as sweet as can be. On my Long Island farm, I had a number of horses, including a few rescues.

A newly anointed horse lover and advocate, Steve had served as a Congressman for 16 years, so he knew a thing or two about politics. I had met him in 2015 at the Hampton Classic, a prestigious annual equestrian sporting event on Long Island. He was participating in a panel discussion for the ASPCA fighting against horse slaughter alongside Georgina Bloomberg and several organizations, including mine. We hit it off immediately. When you start to get to know Washington, you quickly figure out the key players who are pro-animal, pro-horse, and approachable. Steve was one of them.

There were plenty of choices for horses to adopt, too many. In the early 1900s, roughly 2,000,000 wild horses roamed the U.S. freely. Today, there are around 67,000 with another 70,000 in these BLM government holding facilities. Most people are unaware that almost 120,000,000 of their U.S. federal tax dollars every year are going to a program that rounds up wild horses by helicopter and warehouses them in corrals and pastures—sometimes for three or four years and sometimes for the remainder of their lives—all using U.S. federal tax dollars.

According to The Wild Free-Roaming Horses and Burros Act of 1971, "wild free-roaming horses and burros are living symbols of the historic and pioneer spirit of the West. They contribute to the diversity of life forms within the Nation and enrich the lives of the American people. It is the policy of Congress that wild free-roaming horses and burros shall be protected from capture, branding, harassment, or death; and to accomplish this, they are to be considered in the area where presently found, as an integral part of the natural system of the public lands."

This act also put the BLM in charge of managing these wild horse herds. The BLM maintains that they oversee these horses for their health and well-being and the management of the public lands these horses call home--not for the benefit of corporate greed, serving special interest groups such as oil fracking, drilling, and large corporate cattle farming that exports meat to China and other global destinations.

One would think that they would want to give the horses away and help transport them to get them out of these holding pens, but there was bureaucracy at every level. Shockingly the Bureau would rather turn a blind eye as the horses were shipped to slaughter in Canada or Mexico than appear to work with wild horse advocates. Of course, it depends on what side of the aisle you are standing.

This brings to mind an occurrence back in 2009 where the secretary of the interior—who oversees the Bureau of Land Management and is supposed to protect the horses—allowed his friend and business associate in the ranching industry [name purposely omitted] to buy nearly 1800 wild horses over a three-year period for the purpose of selling them off to slaughter. A sweet deal for his friend who purchased the horses from the US government for $10.00 each and then sold them for several hundred dollars each to kill-buyers. The secretary of the interior was even nicer to his friend by allowing us taxpayers to foot the $140,000.00 cost to truck those horses off to slaughter. In the end, the buyer pocketed $154,000.00 while we the people paid $140,000.00 for transportation. Imagine the things that go on that we don't find out about.

In the years I've spent getting to this point I have had my eyes opened to suspicious goings-on at every level. I've grown savvier and achieved more and more significant results. It has certainly been like rolling a boulder up a hill, sometimes by myself, but as the years have worn on, I've grown stronger in my resolve. It hasn't gotten easier; I am just getting better at figuring it out.

Mo went to see Prairie's land, and I checked it out virtually to see where the water and fence lines lay. Though Prairie said she could take 100 horses, we decided that it might be best to start with 50. This would-be part of the proof of concept that I needed to show that it was possible to rehome and rewild horses on native land.

Steve had constantly advised me that the only way I'd convince other politicians that rewilding these wild horses was not only possible but in all of our best interests—was to do it and then have a sheet of paper that proved the results. It was all about the easy, turnkey solution in Washington, but this challenge was anything but simple.

This trip to Standing Rock yielded more than potential land. It also connected me to the film world. I had met filmmaker Shannon Kring through a friend, and I introduced her to Mo. She was going to be at Standing Rock, making a documentary called *End of the Line*, featuring the story of the women at Standing Rock during the occupation. Sometimes meetings happen for a reason. If you believe in serendipity like me, then you also know this to be true. Being able to document our efforts was key. That's where Shannon would come in.

It took several weeks, but we figured out all of the details; I had to do this right. This was not only my dream and goal, but it would be good for our press efforts—which in turn would be helpful in Washington and subsequently good for the horses. I was dotting all my i's and crossing my T's.

Prairie signed an agreement with my foundation to care for the 50 wild horses. The BLM agreed to sell the foundation 50 horses for $10 each. I had no say in where the horses came from or what age they were. They gave me all the older horses that were harder to sell or adopt out from holding pens at a federal penitentiary in Colorado, where the horses were imprisoned. That was fine with me as I knew the horses would have a home and be looked after.

I started to prepare for a trip to Colorado. The team I'd assemble would pick up the horses from the prison and transport them to Prairie's land. I purchased a stock trailer that Mo would be driving. I then hired two commercial shippers to take the remaining 38 horses. We were all rendezvousing at the Canon City facility at a specified time on the day of pick-up. I enlisted Shannon Kring to film the whole thing so that we could use the footage for social media, a documentary, and as part of our proof of concept. It was a whole lot of planning!

We chose a date to pick up the horses, and there was a lot of back and forth with the BLM. When I'd eventually reached a final plan, I called up Dean Bolstad, Division Chief of the Wild Horse and Burro

Program in the Washington, DC office.

"Manda, I am pleasantly surprised. Many individuals have approached the BLM and have ideas about providing homes for older wild horses, but few follow through when they realize how expensive it is to care for horses. I am very thankful for your Foundation's willingness and ability to provide homes for horses and especially for those that are older and not normally desired."

The BLM does allow people to adopt horses out of these holding pens, but caring for a wild horse isn't easy, especially if you're planning to ride that horse eventually. They often need a lot of training.

"Of course, the Colorado facility just wants to give us the older horses that are harder to adopt," I told Mo. "But I don't care. They're older and wiser."

"They'll know what to do with the land better," Mo said. "They've survived this long. They deserve to be saved."

We were to pick up 50 horses from the WHIP program, the Wild Horse Inmate Program, at the Canon City Correctional Center in Colorado. The BLM runs programs at prisons throughout the American West. Inmates work with wild horses that have been rounded up from rangelands. They train or 'gentle' them so that they can be adopted out into new homes. Inmates learn a lot about themselves while learning new skills and the horses gain a chance at a new home and their own ticket to get out of prison. From the healing perspective, horses are man's mirror, so they reflect back to you the good, the bad, and the ugly--the perfect teacher to help inmates heal and rehabilitate.

I'd invested so much in this Colorado trip. Not only the years of my life trying to get to this point, but financially. I'd paid the BLM upfront for the horses. I'd purchased an expensive new shipping trailer, bought six airline tickets to fly to Colorado for myself and a film crew and staff, and on and on.

My assistant Dana and I flew out to Colorado. Mo and his wife Sara Ann drove up from Kansas. Jon, a Native American musician, actor, and model who was performing a song for our music video, flew down from Canada too. We were all meeting in Canon City because the next morning, we'd be picking up the horses from the prison. Separate from having my kids, this was the greatest moment of my life. I was actually going to be doing what I set out to do, begin my journey to help free these wild horses, and to heal people and land.

Canon City is about two hours south of Denver. It's an old mining town with a small population and lots of Victorian and Classical Revival buildings listed on the National Register of Historic Places. Just outside of town are also several prisons. We drove along Main Street past a red brick two-story building dating back to the late 19th century. I imagined the miners and brothel workers milling around outside during the rowdy Gold Rush days. Today, tourists, mostly families traveling on summer holidays, took photos for their social media, and the occasional new parolee made a call from the one payphone on Main Street or grabbed a drink at the local watering hole.

We pulled into the Ramada Inn late that evening. After squabbling and confusion over our rooms at check-in, we dashed to a bar for food and drinks before it closed.

I'm a vegetarian, so I ordered my usual on-the-road house salad and a cheese quesadilla. I'm not a big drinker but decided to order a cocktail to celebrate. I shouldn't have had one margarita because later I couldn't sleep. I was too excited and nervous about the next morning. You know what they say about margaritas; "One keeps you up, but five keep you down."

A little after midnight, I decided to walk out front just to do something with my time. Mo was standing in the entranceway, wearing cowboy boots, Wrangler jeans, and a flannel shirt with his long black braids instantly recognizable sticking out from under a baseball cap.

Mo, or Moses Brings Plenty, is what many people refer to as American Indian. Mo himself just likes to be called Indian. Being American, he says, is inferred, as they are, in fact, the first Americans.

I couldn't sleep. I fiddled with a strand of hair. My long blonde hair is one of my signatures. Running halfway down my back, I've worn it long since I was in my early thirties and can't imagine myself without it.

I remember when I was a little girl, my father used to come home from work and give my sister and me what he called 'the comb test,' combing our very long hair with a comb to make sure it was free of knots. I have kept my hair long most of my life. I guess I feel it is the connection to who I am or the Indian in me.

"It's going to be great," Mo patted me on the shoulder. "Try to get some sleep."

I could tell that Mo was as nervous and excited as I was. As he would often say about our work with Cana, "We are saving lives." That made me a little nervous, too, as it was such a big responsibility.

I looked up at the night sky. I'm always amazed by the brightness of the stars once you get away from the city, and how big, yet close, the sky feels when you go out West. It makes you feel like you are a part of something bigger than yourself. It was a reason that I liked spending so much time in places like Colorado.

I awoke fitfully throughout the rest of the night. My hotel had one of those through the wall A.C. units, and it kept going on and off, so eventually, I just turned it off and opened the windows. In fact, any little thing would have distracted me and kept me awake at that point. I was too excited for tomorrow but now regretted not having the other four margaritas.

Around 6 am, I decided to go down early to see if there was hot water in the lobby. Thankfully, there was. I poured some into my Cana Foundation mug along with my bag of turmeric tea that would hopefully calm my nerves.

I was slipping in and out of consciousness as I lay on the itchy plaid couch in the lobby. Suddenly, 6:55 rolled around. Dana tapped me on the leg. I woke with a start to see Shannon and her videographer Mike Jones at the ready.

"Good morning," Shannon beamed. She had L.A. white teeth and unnaturally blue eyes. I blinked a few times to make sure I wasn't seeing things. Nope. She'd gotten colored contacts since the last time I'd seen her. Must be trending in La-La Land.

A mix of perky and intense, Shannon wasn't wasting any time with small talk or catching up. She was no-nonsense when it came to business, and I respected that.

Like so many filmmakers, Shannon straddled many production roles; a documentarian, humanitarian, and on-camera host. She'd been working for months on filming a documentary about Standing Rock when Mo originally met her. Since he trusted her, I did, too. With shoulder-length bleached blonde hair and porcelain skin, she often stood out in the world that was her so-called beat; Native American issues.

"Well, we're not allowed to film at the prison," I started. Shannon interrupted.

"So, I will film you all here as we talk logistics this morning, and then we can film the drive with you or Mo on the way to the prison. Once we pick up the horses, we can pull over briefly to get some footage of them in the trailer, before we head to the Reservation where Prairie's land is."

"Okay," I mumbled sleepily, glad that she'd already thought through the potential process. I had too many other things filling my brain to take on everything.

"The big thing is that we need to capture your reactions, as well as Mo's, along with footage of the wild horses being released off the trailer to freedom for the first time. We may need to ask you all to position yourself a certain way and film you saying something you say once or twice. You know, repeating yourself for the camera. We've just got one camera, so we need to make the most of it and catch what we can when we can."

This isn't Hollywood, I thought to myself. But then I guess it could have been. We were rescuing imprisoned wild horses and setting them free on Native American land. It was a dramatic story. I had to keep pinching myself to make sure it was all real.

"We have a drone to capture the horses when they first get off the trucks," Shannon started.

"Wait, wait, wait," I finally focused and then snapped, "These horses have just been totally traumatized. They've been chased by helicopters, loaded onto trucks, and driven hours from their homelands to a federal prison. Now we're taking them to a whole new environment. I don't think we need to be buzzing them with drones."

I may have been a little on edge from the lack of sleep. That and I just didn't want to mess up this final part of my and the horses' journey.

"Oh, of course," Shannon took a step back and put her hands on her hips. She gave a look to Mike to invite him into the conversation.

"We'll fly the drone really high, so it won't even bother the horses," he said with what sounded like a Canadian accent, his right hand running through the scruff on his cheeks and chin. With grayish-brown hair and freckles, he had a youthful yet worn look. Even though I would guess he was in his mid-40s, he had the look of a well-seasoned traveling photographer. "But it would be good to capture them running. You know, that first taste of freedom."

"Of course," I said calmly, bringing my tone down several notches to make up for my little outburst.

I looked at my watch. It was already 7:15. Dana was seated on the arm of the couch. Shannon and Mike were obviously here. Jon was yawning as he grabbed coffee. Where were Mo and Sara Ann?

Shannon careened over to chat with Jon while Mike began setting up a tripod, his muscular arms snapping open the legs like they were toothpicks. I pulled out my phone and dialed Mo. No one picked up. I sent a text. Where are you? We're downstairs.

It was, and it wasn't like Mo to be late. He sometimes ran on a slower sort of clock--Indian time as it is referred to--but I thought that today of all days, he'd most certainly be on time. This was so important.

Shannon's voice faded into the background as she continued to talk more about production while her team set up lights in the lobby. They wanted to film us talking during the lead up to getting the horses from the prison. I paced nervously between the front door and the couch as Dana posted to social media. I wondered what was keeping Mo.

7:20. "Just checking back as we're short on time," I texted Mo again. There was a lot we had to do to even get the trailers ready for the pick-up. Mo had to bring over the Cana trailer as it was too big to park at the hotel. He'd left it in a parking lot a few blocks away. I'd hired the shipping company to haul the other 38 horses but still had to check in with them.

7:30. Where was Mo?

"Okay, Manda, are you ready for your close up?" Shannon again flashed her million-watt smile.

That's when my phone buzzed. "I think you better come to my room. Alone," Mo wrote.

My face immediately felt flushed. My armpits were sweaty, and my whole world started to spin. I pulled Dana aside. "What's Mo's room number?" I asked quietly, my heart beginning to race.

"Um," Dana looked in her phone, "239."

"I'll be right back, guys," I chipperly announced to Shannon and Mike as I made a beeline to the stairs. I walked casually through the door of the staircase, but once I heard it close behind me, I bolted up two steps at a time in a panic.

I could imagine my husband and kids back in New York. I hadn't had to leave them during any major life events, but my leaving was always a big deal for them, even now that the kids were in their teens. My husband, Albert, and daughter Sabrina always made me feel guilty for having a life outside of them in general. My son, on the other hand, was always supportive and proud. I could imagine him telling everyone about what mom was doing right now. She's releasing horses in Indian country, while my husband and daughter tried their best to understand what I was even doing. I felt a pang in my stomach as I imagined it. I could not fail at this, but I knew I was about to get bad news.

I knocked loudly on door 239, only to have door 242 open behind me. Dana had given me the wrong room number!

Mo swung open the door with a wild look in his eyes that immediately sent me reeling. With one of his three-foot braids half braided and the other side all kinky and uncombed, he motioned for me to come inside. I could tell that this was not good. This was bad, very bad. I stood outside of his room, glued to the dusty carpet.

"So, Prairie sent me a text and said not to come with the horses today,"

My heart pounded as a wave of flushed heat passed through me.

"What am I going to do with fifty horses, Mo? Fifty horses for which I've now paid. They're mine! My entire reputation, Cana's reputation, is all on the line here."

My comment was met with complete silence. This was a disaster.

2. LAKOTA LANDS

There are only two ways to live your life. One is as though nothing is a miracle. The other is as though everything is a miracle.
~Albert Einstein

I entered the room and started putting my iPhone to work, smiling, and dialing. It's so hard to get people on the phone these days. I probably would have been better off texting, but this wasn't something I wanted to put into writing. I left a more candid and frantic message with Congressman Israel, who has believed in me and my concept from the start. I reached out to Senator Bennet from Colorado but got no further than his secretary. I had so many people waiting for these horses to be released on Prairie's land, from Senators and Congressman to local communities and even the news media. Everyone was expecting these horses to get released today. Most immediately, Shannon and her videographer were waiting for me downstairs. I had to figure something out.

My stock trailer only fit 12 horses. Also, I had hired two commercial shippers who were already on their way to Canon City. I dialed the shippers, and the dispatcher connected directly through to the trucks.

I had to buy myself more time.

"Could you come back tomorrow?" I asked sheepishly.

There was a long pause. I could hear the sound of the engine revving down the highway in the background.

"I'd be happy to pay you for your services today and then, of course, for tomorrow, too." I was grasping for something here.

"Well, yeah, you're going to have to," the dispatcher replied gruffly, followed by another minute of silence and the hiss of his C.B. radio. "I'll have to move some other jobs around but will make it work."

I heard the click after he hung up and immediately dialed back Jan at the prison. She was the nicest woman who truly only had the horses' best interest at heart, but I was wondering how being a day late to my appointment would go down with her.

"The landowner had to go to Rapid City for some emergency family issues, and she, of course, wants to see her horses released," Jan seemed unhappy about the situation but seemed to buy it.

I had brought myself some time with a few phone calls, but meanwhile, I was totally freaking out and punting because this whole thing had become a complete debacle. I had no options at this point, as bringing 50 wild horses to my 16-acre farm on Long Island was definitely not feasible.

In addition to the entire world, what would I say to my family back home? They had been firsthand witnesses to all of the time and money that I expended and friction that had developed over the years about my belief in doing this. I looked over at Mo, whose eyes were now lost in the pattern of the grey textured wallpaper.

My eyes glazed over for a minute too. Separate from anything, this was my life goal and my entire dream. It had been costly; I'd already spent over $10,000 to get this Colorado project set up. Everything had been orchestrated perfectly. This was supposed to be my rewilding proof of concept that would launch everything going forward.

"Mo. What are we going to do? What are we going to do?" I raised my hands to the ceiling and let them smack down to rest on each side of my forehead. I opened one eye to peek over at him. I could tell Mo was thinking about something. He just wouldn't say what it was.

"You know my family has land. My dad has 106 acres." Mo touched my arm to wake me up. I looked him in the eyes. "Let me call my dad. Let me speak to my parents."

I grabbed his hand and gripped it hard, looking through his eyes into the back of his head. "You have to. Oh, my God. We need help! The horses depend on us!"

Mo practically ran out of the room to call his dad. I continued to madly scroll through the contacts in my phone to think of anyone else who could help right now. I called Congressman Israel again as I was so panicked to see if he was able to help in any way-- what that would be, I didn't exactly know. I just needed help and connections! This time, I didn't leave a message.

A few minutes later, the door opened, and Mo sheepishly stood in the entrance. "We can take maybe twelve for now."

"Only twelve?" I smacked my hand against my forehead and sat back at the end of the springy bed.

It wasn't ideal, but it would have to work. It was a further drive to Mo's, which meant we'd need time to organize this new route and plan, as well as work on what do to about the rest of the horses.

I walked downstairs and explained to everyone that we had some temporary issues with Prairie's land and that we'd be picking up the horses the following day. After a slew of questions, most of which I couldn't answer, Shannon and the crew decided to go into town and get some footage and film what they could of the prison from afar. Dana and I made calls and sent emails to explain that we'd be delayed a day in our triumphant 'freeing of the horses' plan. I was exhausted by 4 pm and tried, unsuccessfully, to meditate in my room before resuming work on trying to figure out what to do with the additional 38 wild horses that now belonged to Cana Foundation, and me personally, and were going to be still sitting in prison.

The next day, we woke up early to drive the long, desolate flat road to the Colorado penitentiary. We were now only picking up 12 of the horses, but at least we were getting some. The rest would have to wait.

Shannon started filming us at the hotel that morning. Looking back at the footage, I had the strangest stressful grin as I put our Cana Foundation magnet logos on the side of our truck, opened the door, and hopped into the back seat. Shannon's videographer Mike wanted to film Mo and me during the drive, so he sat in the front to get Mo driving and then pivot to film me in the back seat. Shannon sat beside me.

"How are you feeling, Manda?" Mike asked from the seat beside me. He awkwardly craned around the seat to film me.

"There are other horses there that have been waiting since 2011. 2011! They've been in jail. It must be what people feel like when they go to jail, and they're accused of crimes of which they're not guilty. They sit and wait for one appeal and the next appeal and some miracle to come and say, "you're free, you're not guilty." Because really, that is the truth. The horses are being accused of a crime—of degrading and destroying the land," A tear was forming in my right eye. I rubbed my hands together as a distraction and tried to catch it before anyone noticed

Mo piped in, and Mike swung back around to film the front seat.

"They are figuratively, literally, and geographically in prison, and for a lot of people in Indian Country, we've often dealt with that environment for even our blood relatives. To finally get there and get to look them in the face and say, "Hey, you're coming home." That's what we're going to be doing."

The energy in the truck changed. I suddenly felt good that we were even saving 12 horses today. Sure, it wasn't what I'd planned and hoped for, but we were bringing these 12 home, finally.

Mike asked Mo to slow the vehicle as he rolled down his window. We could see the horses from afar, grazing on brown grass behind several barbed wire fences at the supermax facility. He stuck the camera outside to film them. The cool air felt good. I took a deep breath and exhaled.

Right before we entered the first prison gate, Shannon and Mike hopped out of the cab to let Jon and Dana into our vehicle. They would help load the horses at the prison, and Shannon and Mike couldn't bring the camera inside.

Driving into a maximum-security prison is no joke. I'd filled out endless paperwork for everyone going in ahead of time, sending in copies of their driver's license, front, and back. Everyone had to be cleared by a security check. Picking up the horses was going to take hours.

We arrived by 9 am and were greeted by a security guard who had us take everything out of our pockets and bags, including our phones. We were led through several checkpoints before we got to the area where the horses were waiting. Each horse had a cord tied around their neck with an individually numbered tag. The gate opened to form a chute, and Mo backed our truck and trailer inside. Rustlers on either side with whips and flags cajoled the horses up the ramp that led into the back of the truck. The horses' hooves against the steel ramp sounded like machine-gun fire as they tried to back down the ramp, only to be persuaded back up by a rustler. The scene was chaotic, and the energy; intense.

There was something about the noise that was so disturbing. The horses were panicked and afraid after everything they had been through. I kept trying to send calming energy to assure them that they were safe, but it would take more than a few calming thoughts to heal the trauma they had experienced.

Instead of driving them to Prairie's land in North Dakota, we traveled to the Pine Ridge Indian Reservation, an Oglala Lakota reservation in South Dakota. What would normally take 7.5 hours took us 13 because we stopped several times along the way to check on the horses. Sometimes, we'd find that one had laid down in the back, and we'd have to get them up again, so they didn't get trampled by the others while we made our way down the highway.

By the time we reached Mo's family home, the sun was beginning to set. It was nearing 8 pm, but out west in the summer, it stays light until nearly 10 pm and it's the most amazing time of day--almost like magic.

Mo's Uncle Leonard was there to greet us in his purple t-shirt adorned with a graffiti version of a wolf and a green bandana tied around his forehead. He was much older than Mo, his skin well weathered from a life spent outdoors doing manual labor on the family's land.

He greeted us with two lit bundles of sage. He handed one to Mo, and they gave each other a quick, tight embrace against the backdrop of rolling, honey-colored prairie land that stretched out behind them as far as we could see.

Mo's family's land was beautiful, especially as the golden light of the evening was upon us. I got out of the truck to stretch my legs as Mo, and his uncle walked around and around the trailer, wafting burnt sage into the air to cover the area and the horses in the scent. They sang in Lakota. Scan the QR code with your device to experience the sound.

I could feel the power and sheer presence of the land like nothing I had felt before. I could feel the energy running up my legs from the ground. This was sacred land. Land that held the secrets to the past, secrets to the spirits of the native people. The ceremonies that this land has shared were embedded in its soil. It felt right that this was where we were releasing our first horses. I finally felt a sense of calm and peace about how right my dream was.

Dana and I stood with Jon to one side. Shannon whispered to Mike, who leaned down from the roof of the trailer. I hadn't even noticed him climbing up on top to film us from above, and off in the distance, the sun was beginning to dip below the horizon. The South Dakota sky was awash in purple, pink, yellow, and orange.

Leonard lit a long pipe and passed it to Mo. Sara Ann moved to the back of the trailer with Jon on the other side to swing the trailer's back gate open. Mo signaled to Shannon that he was ready to open the back door and release the horses. Leonard continued to sing a ceremonial horse song.

We shared in smoking tobacco in the ceremonial pipe, considered medicine by Native Americans. I had dreamt of this moment for so long; I couldn't believe it was happening.

Shannon gave him the one-minute sign and motioned for Mike to come down. He shimmied to the end of the trailer and sat Indian style to get a shot of the doors opening and the horses running out.

As the trailer door clicked open and Mo and Sara Ann swung the doors ajar, I was expecting to see a rush of horses flying out of the trailer. Instead, the horses' hooves clattered slowly on the steel flooring. It was a good couple of moments before I saw the first hooves hit the soft grass. Gradually, the next set of hoofs followed, and then another. The first three horses ran off together. It wasn't but a few moments later that a steady stream of the rest of the horses jumped off the trailer to their new home.

"You see a freeze brand right here. Just like us, we have tribal enrollment numbers. They do too. They're given a barcode. That's how they treated us as well," Mo's voice beginning to shake. "But it feels good to see them coming out here. They're home now."

And they were. When they came out of that trailer that evening, smelling the wet dew on the South Dakota grass for the first time, they were finally where they belonged, back home!

"A lot of the horses have been in holding pens for years. They haven't seen this green vegetation. They haven't seen life. They haven't seen rain come down and bring life to this environment. And so, when they step off those trailers, they are finally free," Mo lifted his hands to the heavens, and the horses began to run together further down the hill into the pasture.

"It looks like they're dancing," I smiled. Mo put his arm around my shoulder.

"Good job, Manda," he whispered in my ear.

I could never explain how I felt inside at that moment; perhaps it was actually the beginning of my own sense of freedom.

We released less than half of the number of horses we had intended to on Mo's family's land that day, but the moment and what it represented was powerful in and of itself. We had released them. We had set them free again. Their new journey was just beginning. They would finally get to breathe and truly live life.

It would take another three months before I could get the rest of the horses out of that prison. I spent thousands of dollars to pay for them while we waited on a solution before I could finally get them onto Prairie's land. I had another six that I was supposed to deliver to Phyllis Young from the Standing Rock Dakota Access Pipeline protests. She had agreed to take horses, but a similar situation to that of Prairie arose. I called up Phyllis and was told by her daughter that they weren't taking the horses at the last minute. They weren't ready, so Prairie ended up taking those horses, too.

So originally, we were supposed to have three trucks pulling up to Prairie's land and this big production of releasing the 50 horses to finally run free, and it didn't happen that way at all, as things very often don't.

But maybe that's what was supposed to be. Mo was with me on this journey. Prairie was too, but not at the forefront like Mo. Mo's family's land has a special energy, and now the horses have had babies, and those foals are gaining nourishment and sustenance from Mo's land. By the very virtue of their grazing, they are helping to keep the land healthy and sustainable.

Mo's uncle called him the other day to say that he couldn't imagine what his life was like before the horses came to live there. Came back, that is. Wild horses will wake you up inside.

And that's exactly what I had intended.

3. RESCUE ME

Life changes in the instant. The ordinary instant.

~Joan Didion, The Year of Magical Thinking

Here I am with this nice little life. I've got my two small children and a more-than-comfortable house on Long Island. I'm riding my horse every day, attending horse shows, making dress sheets, coolers (used to bring a horse's body temperature down after a workout), and little matching jackets for the rider and dog. I have all kinds of stuff that I'm doing, yet I'm always trying to find something to do with myself. I wasn't sure why at the time, but I know why now.

All of us, I believe, have a calling in life--a path and journey for which we have knowingly or unknowingly signed up. Whether we find it or not, that's another thing. But what spurred me to start all of this, I can remember like it was yesterday. You know when you have things in your life that are just so present. Back in 2008, I received my calling. It's a calling that many of my loved ones wish I hadn't tuned in to hear. It's taken me away from them at times and into a realm that I can't yet explain. It's on my mind every waking minute. It's something that I know that I have the responsibility to solve in my lifetime. I work at it every hour of every day in some capacity.

It all started when I got an email from my veterinarian, asking me to sign a petition. I was caught off-guard as I scrolled through the attachments and came across an image of a little Palomino mare being led off a trailer into the driveway beside a shabby red barn. The email said that she was pregnant. She was going to have a baby. Along with her came a chestnut mare with a pretty white face and white socks up to her stomach. A sweet Appaloosa had come willingly off the trailer when he arrived at the barn too. Rare, as most rescued horses are fearful during their transport to a new location.

These were horses that Christine Distefano, the owner of Amaryllis Farm Equine Rescue out in the Hamptons, had saved from 'kill buyers,' so-called people who buy horses cheaply at farm animal auction-houses so that they can be sold for meat. They had also sent a video of the horse trailer pulling up into the driveway with this motley crew being coaxed out, hooves sliding onto the pavement of their new world.

I was shocked to read that the horses were being 'saved' from kill buyers. I didn't understand. I didn't understand how these horses right down the road from me were rescued from slaughter because I knew we had passed legislation that had made horse slaughter illegal in the United States back in 2006. By defunding federal and commercial inspections for horse slaughter plants, the Horse Slaughter Prevention Act had forced the closure of all kill facilities on U.S. soil.

Yet, just down the road from my private stables lay a rescue where horses were being purchased up from auctions only a state away in New Jersey. The horses, of course, would be happy to be relocated to the Hamptons. Who wouldn't? But I believed that the slaughter plants had been closed down. This all seemed surreal. I'd been one of the first to sign the petition and had followed the news back in 2005 and 2006.

I sat myself down in the office of my stables on the property of my Long Island home specifically to learn more. I have a beautiful and eclectic sixteen-acre farm about a half hour's drive from Manhattan, complete with brick stables housing a dozen stalls for horses, an equine treadmill, a competition-sized horse riding and jumping arena, bees, wildflowers, and a vintage Winnebago. This is my private farm, and these are my private stables. I don't apologize for this but rather explain it in terms that I've come to understand. From privilege comes responsibility.

For quite some time, I wasn't sure what I would be responsible for, but somehow, I knew it was something important. On the day I received this email from my veterinarian, I took it to heart.

Sitting in my office was usually a Zen experience. Plush brown leather couches accented with tribal patterned pillows are positioned beside a large mahogany desk where I usually work on my laptop. Spattered around the room in various shapes and positions are the seven dogs that follow me everywhere and who I couldn't be without--four German shorthaired pointers, one large sandy rottweiler looking mutt, a small chihuahua, and a chihuahua miniature pinscher mix who is clearly the boss.

If I'm seated behind the desk, I can stare outside at my various paddocks to perhaps see my daughter exercising one of our show horses or others taking a break in the afternoon sun. Behind me is another window that looks into the hallway of my barn so I can hear the clip-clop of hooves on the pavement as a trainer or groom cares for or walks a horse by. The air smells of the sage incense I usually have burning, and there's always good energy, a horse's energy at the ready.

If I'm lounging on one of my couches or the easy chair, I can see outside and also into the stables, which was my situation on that day. However, on this day, the energy changed altogether.

The email had a disclaimer saying that the attached video was difficult for many to watch. I made myself watch it. I made myself because if I were going to engage, I'd have to talk the talk and walk the walk to be the genuine article.

I've been ensorcelled by horses my whole life. Ever since I was three years old and I had my first pony ride down a dirt road beside what's now the Whole Foods off Jericho Turnpike. My father stopped the car on the side of the road, where there were two people with two ponies. The ponies were all dressed up with bows and ribbons and a little sign offering pony rides. In a fleeting moment, my father unknowingly lit a spark that would put me on a path; for better or worse.

It was three bucks, and they slung you on top and walked you up and down a dirt road. It wasn't a glamorous place to ride a pony, but that didn't matter. I knew from the moment I was set in a saddle that I'd be there for life, and that was it. I've been enchanted ever since.

I was in my 40's and lived a good life with my husband and two kids, my horses, dogs, and my parents. It was a small world, but a good world. But, a storm was a-comin'.

I pressed play and watched a few seconds of the shaky undercover video. The footage showed horses in El Paso, Texas, being transported from one big truck up a narrow ramp and into another big truck, their hooves clanking on the steel ramp like a death-row march. A man in a collared grey jersey-shirt with a cell phone to his ear and a long rod in his hand followed the horses, corralling them up the ramp and onto the truck with the rod. The filming was done from a distance, but the videographer shakily zoomed in. I could see beautiful paints, palominos, and chestnuts being crushed into the truck together.

When they couldn't all fit, the man walked down a side ramp and moved back up, slapping each horse on the butt with his palm to move them along into the trailer. These were their last steps on American soil. This was their last chance to try to run, if only they knew it.

The videographer talked to the camera as he continued the drive, following the truck over the border into Mexico. After spending hours on a truck without food or water, the horses were unloaded in Juarez, Mexico. Now they were at a horse slaughter plant. While some are released into dirt paddocks, waiting to be processed, a few others are led straight over to a series of metal chutes. The video showed a horse flailing inside a metal pen as a man in a baseball cap stood over him with a bolt gun. A loud gunshot rang out, and the horse splayed his legs out to the sides of the pen.

Saliva built up in my mouth. I felt a wave of nausea. I hit pause on the video. My palms were wet against the leather as I got up from my couch and paced around the room. How had I been sheltered from the fact that this was occurring? Surely not on purpose. In a time of over-communication, one can't keep track of everything. This was a particular issue. One that most people wouldn't know about. But I was a horse owner and a longtime horse lover. How could I not know that this was taking place? I felt a wave of sickness and guilt.

These were horses being brutally slaughtered, taken from their native home to Mexico to die a horrible death.

I moved my laptop from the coffee table to the edge of my desk and again hit play and almost immediately again hit pause.

If you've never heard a horse scream, don't, it's terrifying. I realized I hadn't heard it before that day. Horses are stoic animals. Their prey instinct tells them not to scream when in danger, but when wounded or in extreme duress, they may let out a high-pitched squeal that I hope you will never have to hear. This was the sound I heard from the video right before the horse went quiet and was swept out of the chute and onto a conveyor belt.

My hands were shaking and sweating as I went back to the text of the email. Unfortunately, this is not the worst of it. The video you are seeing shows horses being killed with a gun. Others are savagely butchered with a puntilla; a short knife used to sever the spinal cord in a fully conscious horse. Unspeakable.

I picked up the phone and called Christine at Amaryllis Horse Rescue. She was the recommended point of contact in the email from my veterinarian as a person that would tell me how to help. I was born in Manhattan but grew up on Long Island, so I'm not one to judge when I say that Christine answered with a thick Long Island accent.

"Amaryllis!"

"Hello, my name is Manda Kalimian. I received an email from Dr. Beth about your work. I wanted to see what I can do to help."

We chatted for some time, but I had so many questions. I just couldn't wrap my mind around all of this. Christine, full of frustration over the length of the call at this point, yelled an invitation to me.

"Yeah? Well, you should come out for a visit."

She told me that directions were on her website and hung up the phone. Not the best customer service, but I understood that people running a non-profit of any sort, and especially one dealing with horses, are short on time.

I convinced my longtime friend, who's more like a sister than anything else, to come with me. Pamela Polk knew horses as well as anyone that I knew. Our families had been friends since she was five years old. A fixture of the Hamptons community, Pamela has quite the pedigree; her family roots go back to President James K. Polk, the 11th President of the United States, and President Buchanan on her mother's side. She's considered one of the top riders in the country and the best on Long Island.

Tall and athletic with long silky brown hair, her skin is always sun-kissed from days outside taking care of horses, dogs and her pet pot-bellied pig. With a confident air, she dons large fashionable sun hats and scarves; Long Island gold coast all the way. She's a horse person through and through. She's also a Long Island equestrian socialite. I prefix socialite with equestrian, as the who's who of the horse world, ranging from fashion designers, to bankers, to musicians, had trained with her. She and I thought very much alike, too, but whereas I was focused on rescuing horses, her true passion was for dogs. She always had a rescue in tow.

Her sister and I were the same age. Even though Pamela was eight years younger than me, we were like blood. If you're an equestrian in the Northeast or maybe in the U.S., you'd probably heard of Pamela Polk. A more beautiful rider and image on a horse you will never see. She'd won hundreds of equestrian competitions and placed in dozens of Grand Prix events; the highest level of show jumping competition.

I'd spent a lot of time with Pamela over the years, especially at horse shows. For years, we'd hung out in the Hamptons on summer weekends and at the Lake Placid Horse Show. On fall hunt days, you'd find us on wooded trails in Bedford or attending The Washington International Horse Show in our nation's capital. Some have described her as a centaur, half horse, half human, as she seemed to meld with her mounts.

At this time in our lives, she'd been helping me with my three horses and a pony that my daughter and I wanted to show. She would help me with horse shows too. For the trip to Christine's, I was asking for something a little different--if she'd make a trip with me to meet some horses less fortunate than our own. Perhaps the truth was I was a little anxious to go by myself, unsure of what I would discover.

There were auction houses all over the United States. The biggest, and most covered in the news, was in Middleburg, Pennsylvania. It's where many Amish would go to buy and sell their stock, and more recently, people affected by the economic downturn went to get rid of their horses. There were random ones all over. One such place, called the Camelot Horse Auctions, was located not far from my home in Long Island in Cranbury, New Jersey. These were the dark places where people turned to when they wanted to get rid of their horse or pony. It's where they went when they didn't want or couldn't care for their horses anymore.

Somehow, mysteriously, someone made a call, and their child's once-prized show-pony ended up on an auction floor. Even more shocking to learn was that many camps sent their ponies and horses to these auction houses because camp owners didn't want to pay to keep them through the winter. They would go to the same auction houses in the spring for new horses for the summer camp season. Collegiate riding programs were part of it too. Getting rid of horses at the end of their useful life. It made me think of the similarity of sending our elders away after they are of no use to us anymore.

It was a sad fact that every horse was one horse show away from the end of the line. It all sounded innocent enough, like they're going to be put up for auction for somebody to buy and end up out in greener pastures or at least a decent barn with water and hay. Unfortunately, many people that actually bought horses at these auctions either took them right across the border to Canada or Mexico to a slaughterhouse, or spent a few weeks or months fattening them up and then doing so.

It's why I ended up buying four horses with a credit card over the phone on the trip back from Amaryllis Farms. I frantically fumbled with the security code on the back of my AmEx as Pamela drove my Chevy Tahoe, far too quickly, down I-495 West from the Hamptons. We were both shaken up following our visit to Amaryllis. The owner, Christine, knew the equine underworld better than most. The stories she told would make you cringe, and they knew her well at New Jersey's Camelot Horse Auction.

Pamela and I drove out in my SUV to Christine's farm in the Hamptons, an area storied for its wealth, privilege, and summer parties. Christine grew up there, though not in the lifestyle that her neighbors enjoyed. However, it was this connection that gave her an 'in' with the sometimes-insular group that roams the manicured lawns and beaches of the well-to-do area of Southampton.

We parked askew in a makeshift space beside an old red barn that looked like it might be held together with toothpicks and bubble gum and opened the door to the sound of potbelly pigs grunting and ducks quacking. A black cat sauntered across my path as I headed toward the dilapidated one-story barn. Pamela followed, clicking the car into lock while trotting toward me in her riding breeches, high boots, scarf, and a button-down shirt. As usual, looking like she just stepped out of a Ralph Lauren catalog. I was in my more faded jeans, belt, and my standard white Gap t-shirt, trying not to trip over myself as I can sometimes lose myself in my own world.

Inside the barn, dusty cobwebs lined the ceiling. The wooden walls were all chewed up, and the rafters looked like they could fall on you at any second. While the structure itself was a mess, each square stall was kept meticulously clean. You could have served dinner off the floor.

We slowly walked down the hall, passing gnaw-marked stalls; the result of cribbing, a habit that many horses get when they're bored or stressed. A somewhat obsessive behavior; they use their incisors to latch onto hard objects such as the wooden doors of a barn stall, then sucking in air. It's a repetitive habit that is difficult to stop and one that has been documented by horse owners throughout the centuries.

Christine emerged from a stall in jeans, a pink t-shirt, and muck boots. She had her shoulder-length bright blonde hair loosely tied back with a hair tie. A strand fell across her right eye as she grabbed a hose to refill a plastic water bucket.

"Welcome to Amarylis; you must be Manda?"

She reached out an impossibly strong and rather wet left hand. I winced from her bone-crushing handshake.

"Yes, thanks for inviting us," I managed to mewl out.

"Thank you for coming."

She looked at Pamela with an acknowledging nod. Though they were both in the horse world, Christine and Pamela ran in very different circles, but everyone on Long Island knew Pamela, so they were well acquainted. Though we'd never formally met, Christine and I knew each other, as well, from various horse shows like The Hampton Classic.

Christine treated the horses like her adopted children. They were more than well-cared-for; with medical treatments, grazing time, training, and love. She was the kind of driven, consumed, devoted, and compassionate volunteer that you often find at any animal rescue organization. To do this job, you had to be a little nuts.

Christine had made a place and a home for old, unwanted horses. Many of them would have been tortured, starved, and suffered without her. She brought them into her little family, which, I observed, was bursting at the seams. There were more horses than stalls.

She rented the Southampton property and somehow scraped together enough funds each month to keep her rescue afloat, even though the

Hamptons was a super expensive place to live and keep horses. She was always campaigning in the local news and at horse shows for donations and volunteers. Having grown up in the area, she knew just how to pull at people's heartstrings. I'd seen her out and about quite a bit but never before paid enough attention to what she was saying. I guess that was another reason I'd missed these bigger issues.

As we walked by each horse—whose name and basic information was written in purple or red marker on a laminated sheet stuck to the stall door—Christine told us about the last time she called Camelot and went to try to save the most recent pregnant Palomino.

"The auction houses think that what I do is a joke and of no value to anyone. They mess with me too. I get charged probably two or three times what the kill buyers pay, and they nearly always try to give me the worst-off horses, even though the other horses are heading to the slaughter,"

Christine said as she opened up a creaky stall door.

"He's Secretariat's grandson, but he didn't perform well on the track,"

She said, giving a chestnut thoroughbred a pat on the shoulder.

"Little Pie. He's only three, so for a year, we'll feed him. His stall is open to a paddock, so he can come and go as he pleases. Hopefully, he'll continue to grow and get healthier and chill out a bit. Then, we can eventually get him a home."

With two fingers, she removed a strand of hay and lint from Little Pie's mane and continued.

"I used to say forever home, but I don't anymore. Too many leave here and circle back. The owners die or fall on hard times."

She pointed to a stunning black thoroughbred in the adjacent stall.

"This one's owner fell on really hard times. She fell out of a hayloft."

She slid her index finger across her neck as she pursed her lips together.

"She died. No Bueno. Her husband couldn't care for three horses by himself, so we took two, and he's got one that he's trying to keep. People don't plan ahead; horses live a long time."

"But I thought that horse slaughter was illegal in the United States,"

I said as I followed Christine further down the hallway.

"American horses end up in slaughterhouses in Canada or Mexico every day," Christine replied. "Every single day. It's the horse world's dirty little secret."

She shot a glance at Pamela, who looked away. I had the uneasy feeling in my stomach that Pamela already knew this information. She stared down at her fingers, stroking the edge of her nail rather than catch my eye for a moment.

The youngest of seven, Christine had been working since the age of eight, giving kids pony rides at Sears while her dad worked three jobs to keep the family afloat. Horses and animals were part of her DNA. They were the most important thing in her life besides her eight-year-old daughter, Rachel, who also worked on the farm. The rescue was a true family endeavor.

Pamela and I slowly walked by the stalls, peering in to see the once pregnant Palomino mare nuzzling her new foal, whose face was adorned with a white blaze. The golden coats and white manes of Palomino's have featured throughout time. Hollywood Western star Roy Rogers' horse, Trigger, was a Palomino. So was Mister Ed, which was my favorite T.V. show as a child. I used to watch every episode that my parents would allow.

"I named her Triumph," Christine pointed to the mare. "She made it here despite all odds."

The whole scene suddenly got to me. Maybe my mind was turning back to poor Mister Ed. What if he had ended up abandoned or, worse, ended up at auction. Triumph and her foal flashed in my mind as part of his family. I clenched my teeth to try to distract myself but couldn't. I covertly swiped a hand along the bottom of my right eye to catch a tear.

Then, before I knew it, I was standing there bawling. Pamela hugged me and patted my back. Christine gave us a minute and headed outside to do one of the million other things that were part of her daily duties.

"It's just so beyond my comprehension. I mean, here's this nice woman, and she has nothing. Her entire world is raising enough money to personally care for each one of these horses," I choked. "Some of them find homes, others she wants to keep, and she's saying they get driven across the border!"

"I know," Pamela tucked my hair back behind my shoulders and moved it off my sweaty neck for a moment, waving her hand to fan me.

"Yeah, and you knew, Pamela," I blurted out accusingly, crying even more.

"Most of us know," Pamela said, gently letting my hair drop back down. "Once we open our eyes to see."

She was right. I had no right to accuse Pamela. It was the elite horse world's dirty secret that they swept under the hay and shoved out with the manure. Maybe if I had taken more time to get out of my family circle, I'd have known, too. If I had, wouldn't I have done something about it?

It didn't matter anymore. Now I knew, and there was no way to unknow it. I had to do something.

I wiped away the tears with a tissue that Pamela had in her pocket. She was always so prepared. I gave her a forced smile and headed out to find Christine. Pamela followed a bit behind.

Christine was cleaning one of her horses' hooves with a purple pick in an outdoor paddock, where even more horses milled about on sand footing.

"Tell me what I can do to help," I asked Christine amid sniffles.

"You have to call up Camelot. A lot of these guys know that rescues come to buy these horses. If they think you're rescuing a horse, they'll want to torture you. They don't want to sell them to you, and they make you work for it; they laugh at you; at us. A lot of the rescues only have so much money, and the auctioneers know that."

She recited the number to Camelot Auctions, which she knew by heart, and continued educating me on what to say.

"They get new horses on Mondays," Christine continued, opening a gate and heading in to catch a horse. "The auction is on Friday. If they're not out by the weekend, the kill buyers come in and take the remaining horses away in trucks."

She attached a lead line to an older looking grey mare and headed back our way. My mind was reeling.

"Many of the horses that end up in auction are off the track; broken down, but young thoroughbreds. Maybe they didn't run fast enough, got injured, or they're just too untamed to work out. Others come from farms and still more came from places that don't want anyone to know they'd end up there; colleges and posh show stables; summer camps that don't want to pay for horses during the winter."

Pamela finally got the nerve to come over and join us, putting her phone back in her pocket, pretending she'd been doing something important. Christine passed us and led an old mare into the first open stall.

"Listen, when you speak to them," she called back. "Ask the man which ones should be saved."

"What?" I glanced over at Pamela, not believing what I was hearing.

"Let me know how it goes," Christine yelled again, vanishing around the corner with a pitchfork in her hand.

Pamela pointed to her watch. She had a late afternoon student. As Long Island's most popular trainer, her schedule was always packed. I threw her the keys.

"You'll need to drive," I said as we once again passed the pigs and ducks and headed to the Chevy.

By the time I slammed the passenger door, I was hysterically dialing Camelot's number as Pamela revved the engine and peeled back onto the Long Island Expressway, stopping almost immediately in traffic.

"What do you want them for?" the gruff man on the other end of the line responded, following my brief request to purchase some horses from Camelot's auction.

I froze, not prepared for this question. Not waiting for my fictitious answer, he continued.

"Well anyway," he snapped back. "I've got four horses for you; if you can come today. You'll need to pay for them now, too, because the action's almost over."

I fumbled for my wallet and whipped out my credit card, not even hesitating. I was credit card buying four unseen horses to save them from the slaughter. It was the craziest purchase or thing I had ever done in my life.

Next, I called my shipper, Gail, who I use to haul my horses to horse shows.

"Gail, I just bought four horses from the auction house in Cranbury, New Jersey. Do you know where that is?"

My voice must have risen a few octaves. Pamela's eyes darted over from behind the wheel.

"Are you kidding me? Oh my god, Manda. What the hell are you doing? Oh, my God!" Gail yelled. "Are you serious?

"Yes," I said emphatically.

I could see Gail rolling her eyes at the other end of the line.

"We'll have to use my truck, and we've got to disinfect after that. Horses from the auction! What are you talking about?"

It was then that I realized everyone knew about this, everyone except me. I didn't want to know how Gail was so familiar with the auction houses, so I just swallowed hard.

I hung up the phone, satisfied that Gail would head out there to pick up the horses. She obviously knew where it was. But today, I was saving lives, at least four. It was a short drive from Southampton to my farm in Muttontown, depending on traffic, which, in the summer, can be oppressive. I barely remember saying good-bye to Pamela as she headed to her car, and I strode back into my office in the stables, my dogs in tow, happy too that I was home.

I set my keys on my desk and plopped down onto the couch. My German Shorthaired Pointer, Willy, jumped up beside me. The cool air conditioning in my office and Willy's licks on my hand must have woken me up to what I'd just done. I had four horses heading my way. I didn't even have room in my stable. Where was I going to put them!

I dialed my friend Karen in North Carolina with a plan in mind. Ugh, she was going to kill me, but I didn't care. I was saving horses!

She didn't pick up the phone.

4. LUCY

"You know, everybody thinks we found this broken-down horse and fixed him. But we didn't; he fixed us; every one of us. I guess in a way, we kinda' fixed each other too."

~Red Pollard, Seabiscuit

Karen had a 50-acre horse farm in the mountains of North Carolina. The type that was always out with her horses. Her voicemail box was always full, so you'd have to call and call until she finally picked up, and it was a slow Southern pick-up; if you were lucky.

Luckily for me, today, she picked up after just six tries. When Karen finally answered, I was running around with my seven dogs, managing turnout, and micromanaging the care of the horses in the barn. I am very in tune with the horses and their needs, so I find myself speaking for them. The people that work with me think I am a little out there, but maybe I'm normal, and everyone else is space-ranging. I'm going with that.

"Oh my god, Karen. I can never reach you," I blurted out, half talking to her while I was taking boots off of my horse.

"Well, hello to you, too."

I could hear the clank of a horseshoe being nailed onto a horse's hoof in the background.

"I just rescued these horses from a New Jersey auction, and I'm putting them on a truck. I'm sending them to you. You have to help place them," I said, matter-of-factly as if it was like asking to borrow a cup of sugar.

First, there was silence, then:

"You're doing what?"

I explained my trip to Christine's rescue and how horses were being brought at auctions and that some 100,000 horses were sent to slaughter each year from the U.S. While trying to robo-dial Karen, I'd already been online doing more research.

"They aren't killed on U.S. soil because our slaughter plants are closed. Most are shipped to Canada or Mexico, where they are 'processed' and end up on dinner tables in Japan, Europe, and Russia," I explained.

More silence. Karen, like Pamela, was well aware already. Most trainers and farm owners knew all about this, evidently.

"Well, I'm not taking any mares," Karen said.

It was not really like Karen with her southern hospitality to be combative, but this was different. I wasn't sure to push her this time. With a little persuasion, though, she did always pull through with good solutions for horses. She'd helped me rehome a few already, including my daughters' show ponies and horses that she outgrew while becoming a taller and better rider.

"Okay, I'll figure out the mare," I conceded.

Karen laughed joyfully. "Manda, this is so, Manda! Or, might I say, Mandaness"

I smiled because it was. I was always cooking up something a little off the wall and, trust me; this journey was going to be quite the ride. I knew it already.

We worked out the details of transport and timing, but Karen was still adamant about no mares.

The horses were about to be on their way to me from New Jersey, and Gail told me that I'd gotten a quarter horse stallion and two geldings (castrated horses), so all boys. Those could now go straight to Karen, but Gail relayed that the fourth horse was a mare. That was a no-go for Karen so that one would be mine.

I told Gail to bring the little mare to my stables and Gail, loaded the mare onto her smaller gooseneck trailer herself and separated the group.

The next morning, I was waiting outside in the hot summer sun with apples and carrots in hand, ready to greet my new horse. Everyone who worked at our stables knew that we were getting a new arrival and where she was coming from, but no one here understood what on earth I was doing or why.

Gail pulled her mud-stained gooseneck into the driveway of the barn. At just over five foot nine, Gail was tall, thin, strong, and very smart. She always wore a baseball cap with her curly, short brown hair sticking out of the back, kind of like a mullet. Almost always, Gail dressed casually with a western flair. She had quarter horses of her own that she showed. Working for a local veterinarian, Gail knew all about medications and her way around the horse world; the good and the bad. In hindsight, I am sure she had a few stories she could tell, but I never asked, and she would probably not tell anyway. She seemed to know everyone on Long Island, and they all knew her.

"Manda, I hope you know what you are doing?" she said to me. I looked at her like one of my dogs cocking my head slightly to the left. Why was she saying that? As she hitched open the trailer door, I pulled my sunglasses back on top of my head. The sun was intense. I had to blink several times to adjust to the darkness inside the trailer.

I couldn't believe what I saw inside. Skin and bones, a little Paint mare, was shaking. She'd wedged herself in the corner of the truck and was scared to death.

Loading and unloading from a trailer are two of the most dangerous things you can do with a horse. You're asking a large animal with an instinct to flee danger, to enter and exit a small enclosed space. Their hooves bang on the steel, and then they are locked inside while it rambles down highways past noisy traffic. For horses not used to it, it can be terrifying.

Working to coax the little mare out of the trailer was a feat. Gail put a lead shank on her and slowly led the girl out, deliberate and easy. As she eased out, I got the first chance to see her clearly.

As she moved from the darkness into the light, I could see that her eyes were severely infected. Puss ran down both sides of her face. Her legs looked like toothpicks, and her shoulder blades were sticking up and so frail. She had two stickers on both sides of her haunches, where a patch of brown turned to white. The number on her stickers read 770.

"It's as if she was a felon," I muttered, utterly disgusted at this horse's condition.

Her coat was a marbled coloring of brown, black, and white with white legs and white across her back between her withers. I could see some redness showing under the white of her coat and wondered if she also had some skin irritation.

"They have her marked with stickers on her ass like she's committed a crime," I said to Gail as I walked around the little mare, running my hand along her back.

"Well, she's scared," Gail replied. "And she recently had a baby. Must have been sold at the auction, too."

Gail led her around so I could have a closer look. I leaned over slightly to see her underside. Her teats were bright red and engorged, still dripping milk.

In her current state, Gail advised me not to expose the other horses to her until we'd done a full medical workup and shots. Cathy, my barn manager at the time, a tough Irish horsewoman who was used to taking care of million-dollar Grand Prix horses, could not understand and had no tolerance for any of this. She chimed in with, "Yes, put ALPO (A brand of dog food) out in the shed. Don't get that thing near my show horses." I swear I must have burned a hole through her with my eyes for that one.

I had a little run-in shed stall in a grassy paddock. I grabbed the lead line and slowly led her out through the grass. She was cautious, putting out way too much energy with each deliberate step. It made me wonder if her hooves weren't properly maintained, either.

Once we got under the small shelter, she seemed to calm down. I stroked her mane gently, tears welling up in my eyes. I didn't want to leave her side. I couldn't find a place for all the sorrow I was feeling from her and for her. The sadness and the pain of what she must have been put through. How scared she must have been following being thrown into a feedlot with a baby, no less, having to protect her young from all the strange horses awaiting their unknown fate.

Horses are sentient beings, making them the most sensitive to all feelings and other's emotions. That is why horses are used for all the therapeutic programs with people. They mirror and pick up the sensitivities and feelings of others. The trauma alone of this experience was unimaginable.

"You're going to be okay, little mare."

Tears were running down my face. I couldn't help myself. How can we, as people, be so callous about other living beings? My lip quivered as I kept whispering it over and over again. I sat on a stool beside her in the shed the rest of the day and into the evening. It was so hot out there that even my legs were sweating; I was drenched, but I couldn't even leave for water. I was beyond parched by the time I could hear the crickets chirping, and the air finally begin to cool.

No one in my house seemed to wonder where I was until after 7 pm when my son stood outside of the stables calling my name. He sounded like a mirage in the distance. "I'm out here. In the shed," I managed to call back. It was then that I was shaken back to reality. What was Albert going to say when he saw this? Ugh, I did not want to go through the myriad of explanations about buying a horse from slaughter and doing what with it? This was not Albert's strong suit. He was practical and always properly thought through each endeavor and scenario. Not quite like me. Obviously!

"Oh mom," Daniel said. He was just nine at the time and deeply into basketball. He had been shooting hoops so he too was sweaty, but I must have looked a mess.

"Uh, we were wondering about dinner?"

"Honey, can you get me some water?" My mouth was so dry. I could barely form the words.

I'd already decided that my family could figure out dinner for themselves tonight. I had a greater mission, to keep this horse alive and well for the evening until the vet could come in the morning.

This night with the horse, I would unofficially start my journey and my first realization of who I was and what my life and existence was truly meant to be. If I'd known all of the challenges that I'd be facing along the way, would I still make the choices that I did? I believe that I had to.

5. HOOVES ON FIRST

Lucy's magic

When Allah created the horse, he said to the wind, I will that a creature proceed from thee. Condense thyself. And the wind condensed itself, and the result was the horse.

~Marguerite Henry, King of the Wind

My daughter named her Lucy. Over the years, she flourished. I used to take her with me to the horse shows as the mascot for the organization I'd soon start, Seraphim12. She'd let anyone do anything to her, making her a great representative of just how amazing a being can be when given a second chance.

At the Hampton Classic Horse Show, one of the premier horse shows of the Long Island summer, and in the Northeast, Lucy would be by our tent. We used to braid daisies and flowers into her mane, and little kids would draw pictures of her. Once I saw the drawings, it gave me an idea.

By that time, I'd started a non-profit dedicated to helping unwanted horses and advocating to save horses from slaughter. Our mission was to create a sympathetic balance between horse and man. We advocated for a shift in perception about their care and classification so that all horses have a dignified life, final retirement, and resting place. Seraphim12 Foundation launched in 2008 with the vision and understanding that humans help horses, and horses help humans.

We started summer camp programs for kids and took Lucy into schools to teach children (and adults) that by caring for animals, and horses specifically, we care for each other. Anyone who's had a pet or loved an animal knows this.

Lucy organically became Serphim12's equine representative. After all, she'd been saved, and what a blessing she was to me.

The kids started to write letters on their drawings of Lucy. Letters to President Obama about how much they loved their horses and how much light Lucy brought to their lives. It wasn't specifically about protecting horses from slaughter, but that was our end goal; to keep it legislated and get horses the federal recognition and protection they deserved.

I took Lucy to the Mets Stadium at Citi Field, where we hosted nights called 'Hooves on First' to allow the general public to get up close to a horse and learn about them in an urban environment. People who grew up in the city may have seen police horses on occasion, but some have never gotten up close to pet a horse and feel their aura and presence. Lucy's aura exuded good energy.

The other horses that we saved that day from the auction in New Jersey found good homes, too. Karen got two of them into school programs, so they were what we call 'school horses' to help kids learn to ride. The Quarter Horse stallion was gelded and went to a nice man who loved him to death. He became his trail horse.

I had started Seraphim12 because of that trip to Christine's, but it was much more than that. That was the catalyst to get me started on my journey, and I believe it was meant to be.

I realized that first night with Lucy that nobody wanted to step up. Horses were being abandoned and disposed of at the auction houses and the slaughter, but nobody wanted to talk about it. No one that was in my horse show community in Florida or Long Island ever talked about it. Nobody wanted to take the time or go out on a limb to stand up for these horses that they claimed to love and who had given so much of themselves.

This was shocking to me. The posh riders and expensive trainers simply turned a blind eye to where their horses went after they finished winning ribbons. Broken, cast aside when they stopped winning and making money. They didn't want to cross the line to learn about what happened next because they knew it wasn't good and didn't want to take responsibility. Turning a blind eye has become commonplace in our world; people not taking responsibility and living in denial.

It struck me as tragic that horses in our modern times can either be worth hundreds of thousands or tens of millions or be thrown out in Thursday's trash. Horses have faced this dichotomy back to ancient civilizations. The fortunes of emperors and kings often rode on the backs of horses.

American Indians conquered the Plains on the 'Big Dogs' or 'God Dogs,' their original name for horses back in the 16th and 17th centuries.

Too majestic to ride at first, horses dramatically changed life for Native Americans. Before horses, Native Americans used dogs to carry their shelters. Horses allowed them to become nomadic and transport large teepees, which would become their iconic shelters. Horses brought wealth to the Plains people through hunting buffalo. They were used to barter and as gifts, as well as in ceremonies. Native culture considered the horses as members of their family and identified themselves as the 'horse nation.'

In our Long Island circles today, horses were seen as a symbol of wealth, too. Riders were held a certain status above many others, and one could climb in certain circles by attending the Hampton Classic, winter parties in Wellington, and summer fetes in Bridgehampton. I'd attended all of those and had thrown many of the best parties, but I had never seen horses as mere commodities.  I had always felt the same way as the native people. Horses were my friends and my family.

My horse, Gin Rummy, had been my first true love, companion, and friend. Later, I'd love another named Mahogany Hall. Scan the QR code to see 16-year-old me with Mahogany. Horses had helped shape my childhood, connect me with nature, and eventually, other human beings. They seemed to lead me wherever I needed to go. It's through horses that I met my first true human love, Roddy Lopez. It was a horse that guided me to marry my husband.

Lucy had now helped me understand that my job on this planet was to save the horses that brought us all so much. Yes, that's a big job, but somebody has to do it, and nobody else seemed to be stepping up.

Lucy came with me whenever I could bring her, and she really got around over the years. At home on my farm, Lucy stayed outside mostly. She liked to meander in the grass with her friends, so we didn't bring her into a stall. Horses that can be outside live best that way, as nature intended, and she just thrived. Birds would rest on her back as she grazed. I had no other horses that did that. She was loving, kind, and had an energy for which to aspire.

They say it is hard to escape your past, which is exactly what happened to my Lucy. It was the middle of the summer and one afternoon, Emilio, who worked in the barn, came running to tell me something was wrong with Lucy, and she couldn't walk. All I could hear was my pulse pounding in my ears as I ran out to her paddock. As we tried to walk her, you could see that she couldn't really pick up her hind legs; she was dragging them behind her. I am not a vet, but you learn enough after a lot of years around the horses. This was not a good sign. It was possibly one of the worst things that could happen to her.

After about a week of blood tests and two different vets conferring, it was confirmed. Lucy had equine protozoal myeloencephalitis (EPM), a progressive, degenerative neurological disease of the central nervous system. Her poor care and a lack of proper worming over the years before Lucy came to live with us had come back to haunt her.

I moved Lucy into the big barn in a stall full of fluffy white shavings so she would be comfortable. It all happened so quickly I still can't even believe it. I don't think it was even a week after her diagnosis that Juan called at 6 a.m. to tell me that Lucy was lying down and wasn't getting up.

I leapt out of bed. As I threw something on, I yelled to Albert to please take the kids to camp; Lucy was in trouble.

I called Pamela to tell her, and we both rushed down to the barn. I opened the glossy wooden door and stepped inside. There she was, my Lucy, lying down amongst a sea of white shavings looking up at me with her big brown eyes. There was nothing to say.

I am not a quitter. I am a fighter and a healer by nature. I instinctively went into fight mode! I ran and called the vet and told them it was an emergency and to come right away. I gathered as many people as I could, as well as all the lunge lines and long ropes that we had in the barn. Within minutes the vet came careening down the driveway. I led him into the barn to where Lucy was. He took one look at her, and I could see in his face what he was thinking, but he turned to me and said, ok, let's try to get her up.

We were prepared with ropes and manpower. We ran around her in her stall, putting the ropes around and underneath her. The vet was directing.

"One two three, pull."

Four people pulled from every side of Lucy, and I had her head. Again, and again we pulled, rocked, and pushed her to help her get on her feet. My commanding determination that I began with now became begging and pleading with her to please, please get up. Lucy was breathing heavily, and her sides were heaving. The last time we tried to get her up, as I was pleading with my girl to please try, she looked up at me, and I knew.

I nodded at the vet, and he did what he had to do so that Lucy wouldn't suffer anymore. Lucy had changed my world and my perspective. From the outside, it looked as though she was so lucky to have been rescued by me, but it was she that rescued me.

Maybe it was just me getting older, but as the years wore on, I'd become much more introspective and globally-minded. My world had shifted from the confines of New York and Florida to history, science, philosophy, spirituality, and, most of all, love.

I loved Lucy so much. Her truth was that she gave of herself her entire life and that, I believe, made her happy. Lucy's amazing energy now resonated within me, an energy with the power to capture the attention of young and old. I felt I needed her to go on now to forge ahead because she had always forged ahead after much greater losses than I'd ever felt.

Once people know you're adopting and rescuing horses, you end up with more, but none that I'd take in after that would be quite like her. Lucy became my beacon, and over the years, I'd take in a menagerie of horses. Many of these would become my show horses and compete alongside horses that were purchased for tens of thousands of dollars.

During the global economic crisis that began in 2008, there was also an unwanted horse crisis. That was when I got Amigo. People weren't just disposing of horses like Lucy, horses that owners felt had no more value. Now high-priced show horses were getting dropped at doorsteps, too.

There was a horse importer down in Florida who had shipped over a show horse from Europe. This is quite common in the world of expensive show horses. He had just been gelded at five years old and was scared to death. They made him jump big for their sales videos because he jumped well and was pretty. He was for sale for $200,000, but nobody could afford to buy him with the market in a free fall. Nobody was buying anything.

One day, Pamela came home from a show with an interesting proposition. She had run into a dealer/trainer. He asked her if we wanted to take Amigo for an indefinite period. She said he was a lovely horse and quite beautiful. She said I could have him for free. I never got a bill of sale that said I owned him, but he came to live with me.

He was delivered to me in bad shape. Amigo was limping as they unloaded him from the truck and into my large brick stables. He hadn't had shoes in eight weeks. He had bone spurs and cysts in his feet. Like all of the horses I've taken in, it was nothing but the best for Amigo; the best medical care, food, training, time outdoors, but most importantly, love.

He became the most amazing horse. My daughter used to show him when she was 15 in the big Hamptons horse shows. People would come running up to find out where we'd gotten Amigo. "He was a giveaway," I'd say, "But we've invested a lot of money, time, and love into him." We had people offering to buy him left and right, and, having heard about Amigo's success on the horse show circuit, the original broker came back to me asking for money.

"Screw you," I told the broker.

I ended up paying the broker a few thousand dollars to make up for the money he spent shipping Amigo over from Europe just to get him off my back.

Amigo, though, like the other horses I'd rescued, was appreciative and grateful. I'd walk through the stable, and he'd nuzzle up to me when I'd visit him. He exuded love.

Sabrina was crazy about him, and he played an important role in her life. Together they made a great show team. At the horse shows, Sabrina and I had a little secret to winning on Amigo. As they were standing, about to enter the ring and jump around, Sabrina would say to me, "Mom tell him the thing." I would then reach up and whisper into Amigo's ear that he was the most handsome and talented horse at the show and point to the jumps in the ring, telling him how great he was going to be. Sure enough, he would walk in and march around the ring as perfect and handsome as ever. They won a good amount of the time.

You give love, and you get love. I'm a big believer in what you put out in this world you get back. It's an energy that feeds you and makes you want to give and get more. It's who we are supposed to be and how we are supposed to operate; from love!

6. GIN RUMMY AND LEMON MOISTURIZER

"No, this trick won't work! How on earth are you ever going to explain in terms of chemistry and physics so important a biological phenomenon as first love?"
~Albert Einstein

I was born in New York City but grew up on Long Island, back when Long Island was more of a sleepy rural outpost. During the summer and on the weekends, we'd spend time in a house my parents rented outside of Oyster Bay on the North Shore. It was a nature lover's dream. We had bunnies, dogs, and eventually, a horse.

I was a typical horse-loving little girl, starting when my dad took me on that pony ride at just three years old. I remember being seven years old and walking barefoot through dew-soaked grass—after an early summer breakfast—leading my sister, Marti, over to chase a rabbit.

Marti is three and a half years younger than me. I don't know what my mom was thinking, naming us Manda Lee and Marti Lou. It was either the 60's or the hormones. It was probably a little of both, but then again, my mom always wanted everything she did to be different from everyone else.

We moved to Long Island when I was eleven. Living there gave me more time with and access to horses. I was riding all of the time. I was what you'd call a barn rat, and I was happy about it. I became even more so when I was thirteen, and my parents got me my first horse.

My father was a hustler. He grew up in the Bronx, spit poor. The son of two immigrant parents, one Russian and one Austrian. They had nothing, as did all the other immigrant families living in the Bronx.

As a little girl, I used to watch my mother, on occasion, make my father what she called 'ballies.' These little dumpling-like things were made out of day-old rolls, cottage cheese, a raw egg, and matzah meal. They couldn't even afford fresh bread back in the day, so my grandmother bought day-old rolls, hard as a rock, and created 'ballies' to feed her children. Necessity is the mother of invention, and perhaps it runs in my blood to think this way as it has been something that has served me well on this journey.

My grandfather was a mechanic and pumped gas. He died of a heart attack when my father was 16. My father had to leave school and go to work, so he could help to pay the rent and feed his mom and older brother. His older brother then went off to World War II.

My father and mother were both survivors and masters of re-creation. They are likely where I got a lot of my resourcefulness and where-withal. I'm always trying to figure it out. If I can't get in through the front door, I'll try the side or the back or the window or the attic. That was very much, my dad.

He rose from the mailroom of a company and worked his way up to buying it, years later. He was an investment banker, and back in those days, that meant stocks, junk bonds, and unfriendly takeovers. It was a whole era where people were making stupid money from all kinds of wrong things. He was like that. He was never like Carl Icahn or any of those big players, but he did well. We had a beautiful house and land on Long Island. I had a horse, and we took vacations. He used to say we lived way beyond our means.

My parents belonged to a country club. They both golfed, as couples did back in the 70s, and my father was a big card player. He played cards in the 'men's' card room at the club. He played for money, and it was quite the cast of characters that joined those games, the same group of men on the weekends and some nights.

I had begged for a horse for years. My parents had me jumping through hoops so they could feel that I deserved one. Finally, when I turned thirteen, my dad organized with the trainer at the local barn where I was riding to purchase an off-the-track four-year-old racehorse. Green as grass and underfed, my dad paid $2,200 for him. I am sure it was split between all the trainers. The poor horse was probably a giveaway.

He came with the story that when they put him into the starting gate at the racetrack, the bell would ring, and all the other horses ran out while he just walked out. But it didn't matter to me; he was all mine! My dad joked that he'd won the money to buy him in a card game, which wasn't too far from the truth. So, the only thing to do was to name him 'Gin Rummy,' naturally.

I kept him at the small local barn where I was taking lessons. There weren't too many amenities, but it had lots of land and a shed row of outside stalls. Gin Rummy was not an appropriate horse by any means for a thirteen-year-old girl. He was a four-year-old ex-racehorse and had no training, no people skills, and there was no way in hell he was going to cooperate and become my show pony. I loved him regardless and spent every day after school at the barn, brushing his coat and teeth and taking care of him. We had good rides and bad rides, but that didn't matter to me. I'd get on and try like hell just to walk him. I'd spend half the time just trying to get on his back. I'm lucky to be alive with all of the times he ran away with me, but still, he was my life and my world. I'd spend hours with him, a young girl's first love.

Every day I'd come back from the barn with a new bump, bruise, or bite from Gin Rummy, and these were not love bites. I tried to hide each new ailment from my mom, but one day, as my paddock boot dragged across the black and white linoleum tiles on the kitchen floor, my mom called me out.

I was trying not to limp, but she'd heard my right foot. She didn't even look up from the fruit bowl she was arranging. It was a weekend, so she was around the house more.

"Manda, what has happened to your foot?"

I stopped dead in my tracks, knowing that if I said nothing, she'd know I was lying, and lying was my mother's number one absolute worst thing you could do.

"I fell off," I replied, thinking she might not think it was Gin Rummy that was the culprit. Remember, I was 13 and in love. At the same time, I was eyeballing how far I was from the chair so I could sit down versus take the hallway to escape the room. I wondered which was the smarter move as I attempted to put some weight on my foot and winced in pain.

"Again?" She turned her head and gave me a sideways glance.

One thing I loved about my mom was that her hair never moved an inch out of place. She had that flipped bob hairstyle from the 1960s, like Jackie O. Her hair was deep red and always sprayed just so with Adorn hairspray, like a fierce helmet.

"What do you mean, again," I asked. Goosebumps formed on my arms as I attempted to drag over a wooden chair from the kitchen table, the legs catching on the tiles.

"Don't think I haven't noticed! Is it time to find Gin Rummy another home?"

"No!" My face sparked its telltale red, while my heart almost leaped out of my chest, as I pleaded, "Please, no."

My mom let this one pass, and I managed, I think, to hide the next few big injuries, but a few weeks later, when the barn called my mom at work to say I fell off again and should get checked for a concussion, Gin Rummy had to go. My parents said they found him a good home on a farm in upstate NY, but the day the trailer pulled away from my stables with Gin Rummy on board, I was heartbroken. I thought I wouldn't live to see another day.

The next day everyone went on with their lives. My mother went to work at her cosmetics company. My dad went to the city to his office without even a thought about me. My sister continued to sing and dance around the house after school as she wanted to be an actress, but what was I to do with myself and no horse.

Having more free time now meant more time to spend with my mother, which wasn't, at the time, a good thing. We never got along. My mother was a hard person. She saw things mostly in black and white and, although she hid it from the outer world, was afraid of everything.

She grew up in Spring Valley, New York, a working-class suburb of New York City. She had a hard upbringing. Her father had Hodgkin's disease. Her grandmother lived in the house and was diabetic and blind. Her mom died at an early age, so the household just generally revolved around many illnesses. Some people try to take illness and hardship in stride, but not my mom's family. The house, as my mom described it, was filled with sorrow.

After high school, mom's main goal was to get out and get away. She knew she needed money and a career to do it. She somehow enrolled at Toba Colburn, a woman's marketing school in Manhattan, and managed to land a job right out of school, working for Capezio, the company that made ballet shoes and dance apparel. My mother had a lot of style and knew how to use it.

She met and married my dad shortly thereafter, but kept working, which was unusual for that time. By the time she had me, and then later, my sister, my mom and dad were doing well. We lived in a nice apartment building in a prime Manhattan location on Central Park West between 70th and 71st, right across from Central Park.

I grew up unconventionally for the '60s. My mom worked all of the time. Our Jamaican housekeeper, Jane, basically raised me. I was crazy about Jane; she was like a mother to me as well as a friend. She had left her husband and three sons back in Jamaica to come to NY to work and send money home to make a better life for her family. So many of these selfless women have made the ultimate sacrifice to better the future of their children. She was that person. Since she missed her children and my mother was always working, we became like mother and daughter.

One of my earliest life memories was when I was sitting in the car at the age of three with both of my parents. We had picked my mom up from work, and I asked her when she would stop work and be at home. "I'm going to stop after I have the baby," she said.

When my sister was born, she did take some time off and did the "Mom" thing, but that wasn't for her. She spent most of her waking hours decorating our house to fill the time. She would go to large furniture outlets, and we would spend hours on end combing around loveseats, hutches, and dressers for just the right piece of furniture for the right spot. Sloane's Furniture Outlet was her place.

Gingham was her fabric of choice. Gingham. Gingham. Gingham. I can't even say it. What kind of a word is that? But our bedrooms and clothing were everything gingham, yellow, pink, green and blue gingham. It was on our dining room tablecloth, the curtains, matching dresses for Marti and me, and just generally anywhere she could place it. She was really crafty. She handmade the headboards for the twin beds for my sister and me. She used a staple gun to make a large gingham canvas. She then traced and cut large flower petals and stems out of felt, gluing them onto the gingham headboard. I can see them as if it was yesterday. Funny the things that stick out to you the most as a child.

Being at home all of the time didn't fit Mom. She became increasingly jealous of the relationship I had with Jane. She was constantly causing arguments with all of us and unhappiness. Her uncertainty of her self-worth or connection to the life she was leading—and the person she was itching to be—was creating a small war within herself. My father, of course, was expecting the glamorous showpiece he married, with his two perfect children and dog, just like the TV sitcoms of the day. She delivered that for him. From the outside, we were the perfect family, but the reality was way different.

Looking back as a woman with two children, a long marriage, and my own identity struggles, I can see it all so clearly now. Women like Jane were courageously stepping out of their comfort zones to sacrifice and do what they could for their families, their inner strength guiding them, and my Mom, anxiously decorating.

She finally got bored with gingham and decorations—or brave enough and decided she had to do something. The stay-at-home-mom stereotype back then was still in its inception. But this was the fire that burned within my mother and the greatest gift she could have given me.

She was just itching for a solution when her real journey began through an outing in Greenwich Village. Mom and her best friend, Sandy, relished in their outings around NYC, but the Village in the '60s was a true adventure. It was the time of Twiggy, Bob Dylan, and Andy Warhol; though my mom was more conservative, she and Sandy kept on-trend.

I remember them leaving the apartment in their striped, and solid-colored turtlenecks and gingham cropped pants for a meal at a new age café in Greenwich Village carrying their small shoulder bags, hair smooth and silky. My mom loved beautiful, creative, artsy things, but especially beautiful natural things. She wasn't a hippie, but hippie-esque. She used to bring in the perfect melon, flower, or vegetable and say in a low, mesmerizing voice, "isn't this beautiful. Look at this strawberry. It's just so beautiful. Nature is perfect." She saw nature as a miracle and always talked about it that way, and it was. She made us see fruits and vegetables through the lens of beauty. She had this art about her.

On this outing with Sandy in the Village, they tried something new called organic food for the first time at an outdoor café. Live acoustic music played across the street, as people pretended not to see who was walking by and what they were wearing or doing while their waiter explained the organic concept.

"Everything you'll eat here today was grown and produced without any chemicals, pesticides, or fertilizers. It's all-natural.

"Interesting," my mom cooed. And she was interested. Her eyes darted back to the menu from the guitar player, squinting in on new words and concepts like macrobiotics, tofu stir-fry, and wheat germ. After lunch, she and Sandy wandered back into the restaurant, which had this earthy vibe all about it. Corner shelves were filled with bottles of natural oils and creams. They were magnetically drawn to this. Being the person she was, my mother sampled all the products, and they relished in the smells and textures. She carefully took out a pen, wrote down the names of the manufacturers on the product labels, and carefully tucked this valuable information into her purse.

The two couldn't stop talking about the tasty organic flavors and all those yummy oils and creams on their stroll back towards home. They began to count the signs outside of hip coffee shops and restaurants offering natural and organic foods, and when they reached twenty, they had their lightbulb moment. They saw the opportunity to be a part of a new movement for health and wondered if this organic, natural food and the oils and products could be incorporated into a beauty business.

I don't know if this actually happened, but somehow, I imagine my mom and Sandy high fiving along Spring Street in SoHo as they agreed to start a brand-new business. Whatever happened next was the beginning of a new movement.

How and where to get started wasn't too difficult as my mom had the names of the manufacturers from the products in the café in the village. The two ran around going to chemists, who helped them mix and test these new, fresh, natural products they were creating. They came up with a corporate name of 'Nutrient Cosmetics' and a brand name of 'I' Natural Cosmetics. The letter I was italicized, so it had a curvy soft shape representing a woman's body. The important piece was what the 'I' represented, and that was for 'individual.' It was to show that each woman is her own individual person, symbolizing her personal journey.

They created four products to start, a strawberry cleansing cream, a lemon moisturizer, a grapefruit freshener, and a honey beeswax lip moisturizer. As Aretha Franklin was releasing the song, Natural Woman, my mom and Sandy were bottling up nature and concocting a plan to make it big.

They put everything into half ounce glass containers with an oval label and a bright green 'I.' They then placed those into see-through plastic envelopes. They created these beautiful baskets of fruit brimming with big red strawberries, lemons, and grapefruits to showcase what went into each product.

Off they went just like a movie, my sister and I watching them depart each day in our gingham outfits as they went to sell their ideas and products to the top fashion buyers and magazines in the big city, New York! Unfortunately, no one was interested. Mainstream media called them hippies and shuttled them back to the village. As they continued to work to find relevance amid the rejection letters and failed meetings, one magazine took notice. It was Glamour.

Shirley Lord, once beauty editor of Harper's Bazaar, vice president of Colgate, and then director of Vogue, met with my mother and Sandy. This dynamic powerhouse of fashion saw a glimmer of something sitting there in her Park Avenue offices. She told them that Vogue would do a small write up and put a sketch of the products with a coupon on a third of a page in the back of the magazine. In the late 1960s and with no Internet, that was how it was done. The two left Shirley Lord's offices and ran to a payphone on the corner of the street to call their respective husbands. They had gotten their feet in the door.

Vogue created the ad. It was, of course, Vogue magazine, and it had to look a certain way.

There was no pay by credit card at this time. People used to cut out a coupon and send a check or cash. The I Natural introductory kit would cost $2, and shipping was 35 cents on top of that.

Back in those days, people must have had grave patience because it took months for the ad to even run. We were still living on Manhattan's Upper West Side at the time. I remember the day our doorman Jonny came up to the apartment ringing the bell. Sandy was there, which was normal. She and my mom were always plotting and planning now that they were in business together. My sister and I were playing cards on the living room's electric green shag carpet, which sort of made you feel like you were on a suburban lawn.

Sandy went to get the door, to see Jonny's arms hugging a large white bag; Sandy called to my mom in the other room. "Rusty!" That was what people called my mom as her hair was rusty colored red. "Your laundry is here."

Mom answered, saying that she was not expecting any laundry. Jonny chimed in with, "No, ma'am, this is your mail,"

He rested the large bag just inside the front door.

My mom looked at Sandy, and they looked at us, and they slowly, untied the top to see that the bag was filled with letters. They were from women who wanted to purchase samples of products from the Vogue ad.

Mom shrieked, jumping up and down and taking short, fast steps towards my sister and me.

"I Natural is officially launched."

She grabbed our playing cards and threw them up into the air. We were officially put to work. I was eight at the time, and Marti was just five.

From that day onwards, playing card games was replaced by sticky tagging and labeling these little bottles. I spent most of my childhood after that either in the house helping my mom with her fledgling business or wandering around in nature with my dogs and pony rides.

Mom and Sandy were glued at the hip. They created a full line of products, including skincare and makeup. They opened their first store on 60th Street between Second and Third Avenues, one shop away from the famous Serendipity, a landmark restaurant known for its decadent desserts. Inside the store was an explosion of greenery, flowers, and of course, gingham. My sister and I spent a lot of time at the store and thankfully also at Serendipity 3. We used to get foot-long hot dogs and their famous frozen hot chocolate. We were sent there to buy time for Mom when she was working late. For us, it was truly a treat.

They expanded to 150 franchises as well as company-owned shops. It continued to grow and make more money, and my father took notice. By that time, he was still doing well in finance, but my mom had started to do a little better and was receiving a lot of attention in her world. She needed financial guidance, and he saw the light or the easy win, which was his game. My father convinced Mom to make I Natural a public company and drained all money out because that's his way, the hustle. Eventually, they ended up selling to Nutra Systems Weight Loss Centers and made a relatively good profit, but oh, what a ride she had on that journey, I am sure.

I'm a Pisces, and so is my daughter, Sabrina. Our symbol is the fish, and we are empathetic, sensitive, creative, and sometimes a little crazy.

My mom's an Aries and an assertive leader who lacks subtlety and tack. Those are traits that have caused me to loathe my mother at times. They are also why I now admire her. It's why people like Jane, who saw the true insanity in my mom, still loved and respected her and would have done anything for her. Jane actually ended up running I Natural's warehouse operations and shipping. She was the only one my mother could trust.

I'd come to know later that, for some reason, the stars and moon would rest on my daughter's shoulders for my mom, and vice versa. It was as if I was always destined to be left out of the female family circle. Thank God, my son would love me.

But as much as Mom and I fought and were at odds for much of her life, it is in her death that I have the closeness and understanding of who she was and a sense of the relationship that I always hoped I would have. Through my life experiences, I have gained understanding and perspective of who she was and how she must have felt. I believe this is common for many women, with one exception. I concretely know the fire and desire for me to understand myself, my path, and my soul's purpose began in 1969 when a little 8-year-old girl watched two friends head out to lunch at a hippie café in Greenwich Village.

Her message back in the 60s and early 70s is no different to now:

to connect with the individual 'I' that we each are, to find our true sense of self, and to stand in that power is what we all ultimately seek. To show the world that true beauty comes from within and flourishes when we understand our innate connection to nature and the planet. These were the messages my mom was meant to tell. To be quite frank, I know neither she, nor Sandy understood the long-lasting impact and importance of their work. Lois and Sandy's journey was one of the first catalysts for the natural skincare movement in the early '70s.

It wasn't until I was in my 40's that I would begin the journey to find out who I really was and what fulfilled and connected me to my power; what my contribution to the world or greater good would be. My mom passed when I was forty-six, as I had just begun my journey. I always felt that she never was made to feel like the smart, powerful woman that she was because of the dynamics of the relationship she had with my father. This always made me sad.

My mom used to tell me, "The world is your oyster. Go and take it." So, Mom, here I go! I am forever grateful that I am your daughter.

7. AWAKENINGS

As long as we know we're trapped; we still have a chance to escape.
~Sara Grant, Neva

All it takes is a health issue to slap you in the face and put things into perspective. It makes you stop and assess your life. Am I living my best life? Am I doing good? Am I happy? Often people turn to God and prayer, promising to do better within their world or the world in general, but more often than not, this do-good existence is short-lived. How quickly we all forget once our crisis is averted. Sometimes, that crisis enlightens you and maybe even sends you on a path you were not planning on taking.

Back in 2006, we were living the dream. I was in my 40's with two great kids. Sabrina was nine, and Daniel was six. The house at our farm was nearly finished being built, and my parents had finally moved in. The kids spent every day with my parents, a dream to have built-in babysitters. As grandparents, my parents were the perfect people. My kids were everything to them, and vice versa.

My dad was a lot of fun. He was always the life of the party, 'Storm-in' Norman' as it were. He taught my kids to play poker and, of course, Gin Rummy. We had a set of gambling chips, and that is how Daniel learned math. My mother would make old fashioned chocolate egg creams, and I would find all four of them at the table every weekend, my daughter squealing with delight at my father's antics, and Daniel covered in chocolate.

I would breeze in and out with my seven dogs in tow to find I was not welcome by my kids, but that was ok; they were usually having too much fun. Honestly, seeing how happy my children made my parents, and hearing my kids' laughter, made me feel like there wasn't anything else in this world that I could do to top that. My parents were perfect in my children's eyes, and this made up for anything that I harbored against them from my childhood.

In October of that year, my mom began to feel sick. She had been fine up until a few weeks before the diagnosis, and then her condi-tioned worsened hastily. She had liver cancer just like her mom; she was 78 at the time. We were all devastated. Remember, she grew up in a household with parents who were always sick. Her mother died in her late 40's of colon cancer that spread to her liver, and my mother had long ago convinced herself that she would die the same death as her mother. She was absolutist about this and so many things. She spent her life in fear of getting sick. Evidently, it would become her self-ful-filling prophecy.

The doctors found lesions all over her liver. It was Thanksgiving— my parent's favorite holiday—By the time all the tests and diagnoses were made. Needless to say, it was the darkest of holidays that year. My mother wasn't told how sick she really was; only my father and I knew, which made it even harder. We sat at the table, trying not to cry, know-ing that this would probably be her last Thanksgiving.

Lots of treatments were offered, but we knew those would only buy her a little time. We picked some of what we thought were the best. I wanted to do everything we could to buy my mom more time and quality of life. I am a fighter and an optimist, but more than that, I truly believe in miracles.

The mother of one of Sabrina's friends had breast cancer around the same time. I had run into her at school, picking up the kids. As moms do at pick up, she was talking to me and asked me if I knew about Reiki or energy healing. I did not. She explained a bit about it and her Reiki healer, Susan. She raved about her and told me that she wasn't sure she would be ok if it weren't for Susan. This piqued my interest and resonated with me in a different kind of way. I did some of my own research. I thought, "why not?"

Reiki comes from the Japanese words 'rei,' which means universal, and 'ki,' which means life energy. A universal life force energy is what we are all made of and what keeps us alive. It emerged in Japan and spread to the West in the late 1930s and '40s. This universal energy, or life force, in Reiki is also found in Tai Chi and other alternative practices. While not scientifically proven, many people believe that Reiki can help people heal, reduce anxiety, increase circulation, along with other benefits.

My mother had started her chemo, and it was hard on her. After some deliberation, I picked my moment carefully and made my case as to why she should come to see Susan, the Reiki healer. It didn't go over too well at first. My mom was totally opposed to it, but, finally, I just said it. "You're going to go; you have nothing to lose."

It took forever to get Mom anywhere by this time because she was so sick from both cancer and its treatment. She was always exhausted, but she still insisted on walking. Wheelchairs or walkers were out of the question. Just a few steps and she'd need to sit down, so we'd spend about a half-hour getting from the living room to the car, even if I parked it right outside of the front door. I didn't care how long it took. I would have done anything to help her feel better at that point.

After the first visit, Mom was a convert and started to see Susan regularly. In an unexpected turn of events, she would get excited waiting for her next appointment. My mother and Susan became good friends, and Susan became vested in healing my mom. I carefully watched the process and, over time, had several conversations with Susan until one day, I asked if I could come in for a session. "Yes, it will be your turn soon; I am supposed to work with you," Susan replied in her soft-spoken way.

Hmm, what did that mean, I wondered. Now I wanted to go even more. A few months later, she called me to tell me she had an opening; I guess it was my time to go. I remember my first time walking into her house and her Reiki treatment room for my session. The smell of incense wafted through the air as I lay down on a massage table in Susan's small office, surrounded by violet-colored walls and candles; all very Zen.

Our sessions would always start with a bit of conversation about life and what was happening for me in my world. Susan never played music, though some Reiki practitioners do. She would then take a moment to prepare herself and get in the zone, hands clasped, eyes shut. She would move her hands around my body, stopping and resting them on certain places that I guess called to her during the session. Each session, I would float away somewhere and always wake up feeling uncommonly refreshed.

Mom would never talk about her sessions or what she and Susan talked about, but she went twice a week during her cancer treatment. One day she came home with Louise Hay's book, *You Can Heal Your Life*. Her bookmark was a picture of my sister and me when we were little. That book has been my guide ever since. When mom finished her chemotherapy, we had to wait a bit before she could be retested. When she finally had her MRI, they couldn't believe it. I remember being in Dr. Tomao's office at the Monter Cancer Center on Long Island.

"Mrs. Muller, the tumor in your colon is completely gone, and all the lesions in your liver seemed to have cleared, with the exception of two small spots." Dr. Tomao said with some surprise. "Whatever we, or you, are doing, is working."

"Must be the chemotherapy," Mom winked at me, smiling.

I squeezed her hand. I didn't care how or why. We never talked about it, but we both knew. I believed in Reiki. The concept that we each have the power to heal ourselves is our God-given gift. Our ability to channel life force energy for ourselves, and to help heal others, is remarkable.

Mom gained more time, and that year was a big one. We had set certain benchmarks that had to be met. My parent's 50th Wedding anniversary was in April, and that was our goal, that she would make it to see her 50th. My sister got married, and she and my dad traveled. They saw my sister and her family often. We all spent holidays together and ate delicious meals, but most importantly, there were card games, egg creams, and laughter again, for a little while longer anyway.

I always did think that it was odd that my mom had two lesions left after the energy healing sessions. Those two stubborn lesions just wouldn't go away, but maybe that was my mom's doing. You see, we absorb all of our emotions inside our bodies. Each negative emotion creates physical ramifications. Fear, anger, resentment, etc. is cancer for the body. Holding onto these negative thoughts can, and will, eventually take a toll on our physical being.

In the end, my mother had two issues in her life that she refused to resolve. One was her issue with her sister. The other was not forgiving my father for something he had done to her early in their marriage. To this day, I wish my mom had tried to at least let go of those feelings before her passing. I guess she just couldn't.

I was 46, Sabrina was 11, and my son, Daniel, was 8 when my mom died, and our whole family structure fell apart. My father could not be without a woman. My mom wasn't even gone, and they were lining up around the block for a chance at him. My mom and I had many conversations at her bedside before she passed. She had told me that this would happen when she was gone, and she trusted I would make sure the family stayed together. But 'Stormin' Norman' had other plans and almost immediately found someone new and went off to lead a second life, one which didn't include us.

I loved my dad so much for all of my life. As a child, I used to think that if it were possible for my mom to fire me as a daughter, she would. I felt I could never live up to her expectations of me, but my dad and I were like two peas in a pod. I was devastated.

Dealing with my mom's passing was hard on the entire family, but especially my daughter Sabrina. It was 2008, and the market and economy 'tanked,' as Albert would say. My whole world was coming unhinged. I was so stressed after losing my mom and then, for all intents and purposes, losing Dad as well. My husband was completely freaking out about work all the time, and I was trying to help my daughter, who was completely lost without her grandmother. On top of that, my poor little Daniel couldn't understand where his grandfather went and why he had forgotten his birthday. I was drowning.

My connection to the spiritual understanding of things came easily to me, so I worked to find a place to channel that. We called it the yellow room. It felt like coming home.

I had created my own little Zen space in the house. It was my sort of hideaway or, 'she-shack.' All of my private moments and my meditations would happen there. I remember one night going in and hysterically crying. I couldn't breathe. I thought I was going to die. My heart was broken. I was completely lost.

I am innately a doer and a healer. I heal and help everyone, and here I was, not knowing how to help myself, let alone anyone else. I stood by a window and pleaded for help. Not necessarily to God, or anyone in particular, but to the universe at large; whoever was listening. I just felt as if my soul was going to shrivel up and die.

I lay on the floor in the yellow room, gasping for air. I couldn't see where I was going; I didn't know who I was supposed to be. I ached for my children and longed for my mother. I wanted to pack a suitcase and run away, but I was trapped!

The year went on a bit dismally. I was so sad. Had it not been for my horses, I don't know how I would have gotten through. At my yearly checkup, my doctor discovered a cyst on my ovary, which I'd have to have removed. All I could think about was that I was the same age as my mother had been when she had her hysterectomy to remove a cyst. My grandmother was this age when she died. I flashed forward to the end of my own, potentially short, life. Would I have the same early and excruciating demise as my grandmother, and then my mom?

I continued to see Susan, vowing that I wouldn't die like my mom and her mom. I could change my destiny. It wasn't going to be written for me. I would architect my future. For the two weeks before my surgery, I went as much as I could for Reiki. I thought that if I could make the cyst go away, I wouldn't need the surgery.

I was working with Susan and putting everything I could into focusing on getting better. I was looking at all my issues and working through them at lightning speed. I was supposed to have the surgery right away because this cyst was quite large. My gynecologist said it was the size of a golf ball. How I couldn't feel it, I was not sure.

My doctor's mother passed away before my surgery, so my surgery got delayed by two extra weeks. I had an additional two weeks to try to shrink this cyst. I continued to work on personal issues from my youth, issues with my mom and my sister. I pushed the energy and healing as hard as I could.

When I finally had the surgery, I was bewildered to find that the cyst wasn't smaller; it had tripled in size. It had been the same size for nearly a year, but now it was as if I filled it with all of the stuff that I wanted to get rid of, and it was huge!

On the day of my surgery, interns and other doctors who had seen this cyst kept coming in to congratulate me. No one could believe I was fine. When they took it out, they said it was the size of a small grapefruit.

No one understood how I couldn't feel it. It was so big, but I understood now. I was grateful and empowered at the same time. From that moment, I decided that I wasn't going to live my mother's life or die her death. It was just not my destiny. More importantly, I came to the conclusion that I could decide for myself my relationship with the universe and my life. This was my journey. Perhaps that is what Susan meant when she had said she was supposed to work with me. I have an important role to fill in my lifetime; I just didn't know how important, at the time.

I'd read about a native man named Stanford Addison, who was supposed to be a shaman out in Wyoming. He had been in a wheelchair for the past twenty years, following a car accident at the age of twenty. Stanford had tried to commit suicide shortly after and then tried to get other people to kill him, but it never worked. In realizing how broken he was, he began for the first time to communicate with horses. Stanford scoffed at the word 'horse whisperer,' but he was able to connect with horses and heal people in an unusual and real way.

It took me a year to find someone connected with him, and he died shortly before I got to go. Susan was supposed to come with me. She said it was my fault that we never met him, as we didn't try to go sooner. I saw it differently. Perhaps I was not supposed to meet him.

I decided that I needed to go out West anyway. The mountains were calling my soul. It was like I needed to go to a place I knew, like going home. Even now, writing about The West feels like home. I thought, if I could feel the mountains and see the land in person, some magic would be revealed, and I could heal, and in turn, heal the horses. I wanted to feel the energy and find a place where land could be given back to the horses. I felt that a big part of this journey for me was freeing the horses. If they were free, then I would be free in and of myself.

I wasn't just going out West to breathe the fresh air and frolic in the mountains. I was going to catch my breath by focusing my energy on something else, something that was inside of me, my path. I kept hearing my inner voice saying, "To save the people, we have to save the horses and to save the horses, we have to save the people."

If we save the horses, we are saving ourselves as human beings. It's synonymous. It would be a year later that I'd truly come to understood what that meant. I was traveling out to Wyoming to search for land, but I was also searching or longing for something within myself.

Native Americans innately understand sustainability and have a deep connection with nature. My feeling was that, because the wild horses evolved as a globally native species, the same as the native people, they share that energy and understanding. They are the original life on the planet, as I would later come to understand from my friend Mo. The horses carry the original teachings of the creator. Who would understand how to work cooperatively and live together with the planet better than indigenous native people and wild horses?

For my first two trips, my friend Rebecca and I flew through Denver to Jackson Hole. It's one of my favorite airport landings on the planet. You emerge from the clouds in a bowl surrounded by the Grand Teton Mountain Range's icy peaks. It's incredible.

The drive from Jackson to Riverton and the 2.2-million-acre reservation takes about three hours. At the halfway point, you pass through the small old western town of Dubois, known for its longtime dude ranches and old saloons. It's a quintessential Western drive.

On the first trips, we stayed at the Holiday Inn, Riverton, and mixed visits to local galleries, museums, and attractions with volunteering at a local horse camp for kids. After a few trips with Rebecca, I felt comfortable enough to try to make a trip by myself. I thought it was important to do that because I'd never really traveled alone.

I was super nervous the day I arrived in Jackson Hole. I hired a driver to take me to Riverton, and from there, I rented a car. I don't know what it is, but growing up in New York, driving out West makes me more than a little nervous. I could drive all day in crazy Manhattan traffic or on the Long Island Expressway but put me on a desolate rural road in Wyoming, and I'm freaked out beyond comprehension. I needed to learn to be ok alone, with myself and know I could be self-sufficient. What if I had a breakdown on my way down from Jackson to Riverton. There'd only be bison out there to help me! 'Toughen up,' I had to remind myself. I sounded like a lady from the North Shore of Long Island, which I was.

When my driver let me off at the rental car dealer in Riverton, I started to get nervous. It was a chilly fall day, and yet my hands were sweating as my SUV pulled in. As I put the key in the ignition, my heart started to beat a little faster. I realized that I was alone in the wilds of Wyoming.

"I can do this," I said aloud, as a country station ripped from the stereo speakers. I turned the volume down and pumped my hands on the steering wheel. "Woo hoo!" I was off to the races, and it started to feel good! Freedom, wide-open spaces, and my soul felt alive!

That was my first solo trip to the reservation, and I started to dive deeper into life on the Rez. It opened my eyes to a whole new world that I'd never seen. As I got deeper into it, I was introduced to issues that I'd heard about but never experienced: extreme poverty, drugs, disease, and the heart-wrenching inequality Native Americans face. Women are a target of abuse, and many children grow up as orphans.

I decided to try to start an educational program to promote youth and horses. I bought supplies for fencing and helped locals section off lands so their horses could graze freely in the winter. It was hard work.

I was constantly searching for land, too, driving around on my own and hopping into cars to see people's properties and places. I was on a quest to understand the challenges of life on reservations and form bonds so that I could eventually find land where we could place wild horses being held by the BLM.

After leaving my family for about six or seven trips over eighteen months, I finally realized I wasn't getting anywhere. Every time I got there I was starting over. It was like being on a hamster wheel. I saw that there wasn't enough that I could do that would make a big enough difference. Trying to save the world one horse and young Indian woman at a time wasn't going to be enough. On my final trip, I cut my time in Wyoming short and flew back to New York, feeling ridiculous. I was entirely frustrated and defeated. I was done with Wyoming. My time at the Rez was over. I felt more confused than when I started Seraphin 12 years ago. I decided that the universe had picked the wrong person for this job. I had failed miserably. I quit my spiritual day job and dissolved my foundation. I told Albert I was done with it all. Albert was relieved. I was once again lost.

8. MOSES BRINGS PLENTY

Wabluwaste Kta cha wowas' ake bluha
~ Lakota
"I have the power to create change"

There are no accidents in life. If you put out the energy for whatever it is you want, opportunities will come to you. It's just not always exactly what or how you think it will be. That is exactly how I met Moses Brings Plenty, a Lakota Sioux spiritual leader, teacher, and actor. Mo, as he likes to be called, grew up on the Pine Ridge Indian Reservation in South Dakota. Mo would come to be a close friend and teacher, and I would realize we were kindred spirits on a journey.

Mo's Lakota name means "He catches the horse." There are no accidents.

It was 2015, and marijuana had become legal in various states. The Cannabis industry was taking off. People were referred to as growers, and native communities, being sovereign nations, were looking to cash in. Through some friends in real estate, Albert learned of a business opportunity in Colorado, a commercial office space specifically for growers. As he toured commercial Cannabis operations, he was introduced to a woman that was an investor. From the moment she spoke, it was apparent to Albert that she and I had a lot in common with our out-of-the-box free-spirited thinking.

He rushed to call me to let me know that he had connected with a woman named Joan that I was going to love.

"She's just like you."

"What does that mean." unsure of the connotation.

"You know. Spiritual and all that," he said proudly, feeling as though he had just won the lottery.

I knew that meant that she was a little kooky, but I got it.

"She was a big wig at Aveda skincare."

Now I understood. I desperately needed help for Naturally Considerate, my brainchild, and a company that I had been brewing for years! It was the absolute continuation of my mother's 'I' cosmetics. I had started a natural skincare line, and my 20th-century spin was the personal rewilding message. Proceeds from sales were to go to Cana Foundation. It was my way of creating awareness and connecting the importance of saving the wild horses and our lands while reaching a broader demographic. The goal was to give people a greater understanding of our overall connection to nature and all things through each individual's rewilding journey.

I had created six products, including a bundle of sage collected from the Navajo reservation in Arizona. Everything was organic and produced in a naturally considerate way for the planet. Your kit included a groovy pamphlet with instructions on having your own personal rewilding connective moment for your growth and well-being, a small turquoise horse fetish, and a feather charm. I just loved everything about it, and it felt so Lois and Sandy. Albert used to joke that I was 'Cosmetic Royalty.'

It was a great idea, and the packaging and product are lovely, but I am not Lois, and I guess lighting doesn't always strike twice. Getting this off the ground on a wing and a prayer was impossible. Albert felt that Joan, with her experience, could help. She was quite the operator, and as it turned out, she did more harm than good, but it also turned out that Joan lived in Kansas about an hour from Mo.

A few months earlier, I worked on a photo shoot at my Long Island farm for Naturally Considerate. I was looking for a Native American male model and given a few different photos from a casting agency to find the right fit. One stood out. I asked for a call with Jon, whose profile said he lived in Canada and was a member of the Keeseekoose First Nation in Saskatchewan. I hired Jon on the spot, and we set a date for our shoot.

Two weeks later, Jon flew into JFK airport, and I went to pick him up. I was so excited to meet him. As I pulled up to the Delta terminal, I was immediately struck by this very handsome American Indian man with silky black hair tied back in a bun.

I pulled up and yelled out from the window, "Jon?" He looked at me, nodded, and quietly answered, "Ya." He hopped in the car. As we drove back to the farm, I was chatting away, peppering him with questions and making small talk. He is a man of few words. I can only imagine what he was thinking. Then all of a sudden, he blurted out.

"I just finished a movie. I just did a docudrama that Robert Redford produced called the American West on AMC. I played Crazy Horse, our people's greatest warrior." He pulled out his phone and started showing me pictures of him on-set. There he was in full native wardrobe sitting on a large chestnut horse, his long dark hair loose around him. It was really beautiful, and the energy of it was palpable.

As I tried to keep my focus on the road while glancing at his iPhone, Jon scrolled through images stopping at another one. He was standing next to a beautiful tall native man with braids that looked like they were at least five feet long.

"Who is that?" I slid one hand from the leather steering wheel and pointed to the man in the picture.

"My brother Mo. Moses Brings Plenty. He played Sitting Bull in the film. We became very close during the filming. He took me under his wing."

I smiled, thinking back to the various mentors I'd had in my life during challenges.

The shoot with Jon would go on to run smoothly. It was a pleasure to work with him. Joan was in her hometown of Kansas during the shoot, so she never got to meet Jon.

It just so happened that a few weeks later, as I shared the photos from the photoshoot with Joan on a catch-up call, she told me about a native man that lived in Kansas who was an actor that she thought could be helpful for the horses. After she went on and on about how handsome he was, she finally blurted out, "And his name is Moses Brings Plenty."

"Wait, wait, wait; what?" I almost dropped the phone. Was this the same Mo about whom Jon had already told me? It had to be. How many Moses Brings Plenty could there possibly be?

Joan confirmed that it was. He was an actor, too. I knew I had to meet him; I was supposed to meet him!

She offered to introduce me, but I wanted to wait until I could come out in person. I don't like someone else sharing information that I can communicate directly, if I can help it. I feel it makes for a better relationship later on.

I did a little digging on Moses Brings Plenty. For some reason, I just knew we'd work together.

I went back to Jon and shared that my friend Joan happened to know Mo, too, and thought I should meet him. Jon offered to make an introduction for me to Mo. I felt that an introduction coming from Jon would give me more credibility, and it sure did. Mo couldn't have been nicer and more pleasant when I called him. I explained the vision of what we were working on and that I needed help from someone in the Native American community to secure land and introduce the idea of rewilding formerly wild horses onto native lands and reconnecting the people back to the horses, in the physical and spiritual sense.

Ever since I'd adopted Lucy years ago and gone on to start Seraphim12, I had been educating myself on the newest issues relating to horses and had ideas for ways to fix them. Wild horses living on public rangelands have been trapped in a land grab, mismanaged by the Bureau of Land Management for ~50 years. They've become the collateral damage of the cattle lobby's veracious appetite for America's public rangelands. With the BLM holding tens of thousands of horses in taxpayer-funded holding pens, tens of millions of taxpayer dollars were being wasted each year, and the horses—and we taxpayers—were the worse for it.

After deciding to give up on Seraphim12 a few months ago, I woke up one morning realizing I couldn't turn my back on who I was; on my truth. I had to be true to myself, and that meant I was not a quitter. I kind of threw myself back in the saddle. I rebranded my foundation and called it Cana. Through it, we would work to unite wild horses through rewilding initiatives that allow them to live free while restoring an environmental and spiritual balance and bringing socio-economic opportunities to native communities. We also proactively worked to change legislation to support humane alternatives to managing our wild horses. It was a big mission, and a key component was working on getting wild horses out of BLM holding pens and onto American Indian lands. Now I just needed to find land.

I had failed miserably to secure land in Wyoming with Seraphim, but now I was back. It was a new chapter, with the newly formed Cana Foundation and Naturally Considerate.

Mo and I made a date for me to come out and visit him on his ranch in Kansas. I planned to bring Jon, who I'd grown fond of since he came to my Long Island farm for the Naturally Considerate photo shoot. Joan, and my assistant, Dana, also joined us.

We flew to Kansas City early spring of 2016 and drove through flat plains and farmland for about an hour to reach Mo's home.

At Mo's beige, wooden, ranch-style home, we were greeted by ducks and ponies as we exited our rental SUV. As Mo headed towards us, he seemed larger than life in a blue plaid button-down shirt, jeans, and baseball cap. His two long black braids ran down past his hips.

"You know, a lot of people contact me to help them with the horse issue because of my past and my connections. I always say, 'If you want me to help you, come and see me.' They never do. I always thought the person who actually comes to see me would be the person I will work with, and you are here, all the way from New York!"

He threw his hands in the air, laughing, and immediately gave me a big bear hug. Well, there are no small bear hugs. So, a bear hug. It felt so good. Like we'd known each other in a past life or something.

Mo's wife, Sara Ann, strode out of their front door and down the sidewalk to meet us. Only partially native, those attributes showed through in her piercing blue eyes and beautiful tan skin, which juxtaposed her long, light-brown hair.

Mo's Kansas home is a gathering place for his nephews and neighbors and all of their pets and friends, so it is constantly busy.

I'd learned from my time in Wyoming that when you go to visit with Native Americans, it's customary to bring food and gifts. I'd brought three little bracelets made of rose quartz for Sara Ann and a beautiful crystal for Mo. We had stopped at Whole Foods in Kansas City. Since I don't eat meat, we'd brought additional food for lunch; bread for sandwiches, turkey, cheese, chips, and salad.

There's no schedule when you're on Indian time. We arrived at 11 am, ready for a day at the ranch.

After we'd gone through the formalities, Mo said, "Come. Let's speak. We will meet in the traditional way of our ancestors." I intuitively knew that Mo understood I was coming with a message from the spirits, the horse spirits.

He led me into his backyard, where a large white canvas teepee stood out amid the green grass covered in virgin dandelions. The wooden poles sticking out of the top reached into the grey, cloudy sky. For the Lakota, the tipi has been significant throughout history. The main living structure for tribes of the Great Plains that hunted buffalo, the tipi crosses over from the regular world to the cosmic world. The pattern of the circle, significant in native cultures, has no beginning or end. The tipi is a realm for vision quests, fasting, and prayer.

"The hoop of the skirt represents the circle of life," Sara Ann handed each of us long skirts to wear into the teepee. "Wearing a skirt also helps the spirit world recognize you as female. It is your personal teepee."

Joan, Dana, and I put on the long skirts over our jeans and followed her through the open flap. Inside Mo's teepee, the ground was covered in buffalo skins, and on one side was a ceremonial chair and buffalo skull. In the middle, there was a fire pit. The women all sat together on one side, and the men, Jon, Mo, and some of Mo's relatives, were across on the other. The smell of burning wood and sage wafted throughout the teepee. I had to pinch myself. I never felt more comfortable in a place. I knew exactly where I was. It was as if I'd been there before, in another time and place. Mo sat with his legs crossed and prayed.

"Oh, Great Spirit, whose voice I hear in the wind, whose breath gives life to all the world, hear me; I seek your strength and wisdom." 'What can I do for you; why have you come?'" Mo asked, looking straight into my eyes.

"I had a vision, and this was what the Spirit told me. 'To save the people, you have to save the horses, and to save the horses; you have to save the people. It is synonymous,' I need your help in this important endeavor."

Mo nodded and kept listening. Mo would later teach me to sit back and listen and let the other person do all the talking. In this way, their truth would be revealed.

"My plan is to rehome and rewild formerly wild horses on native lands. I know you've done a lot of advocacy work for the Lakota people, and I understand your ties with horses. I want to help the horses and the people by bringing horses back to native lands, eventually creating educational programs, infrastructure, health care, the entire thing." I told him about my time in Wyoming with the Arapaho and how it didn't work out in the end, but I didn't believe that it was for nothing. "I received an education about life on the Rez, land rights, and how to get things done in Washington and out West. I know I'm a blonde woman from Long Island and that it's hard to take me seriously when I say that I know things that I have no right to know, but I just do, and I can't explain it. It comes from deep within me. I'm committed to bringing the horse back to its homeland on native lands. I feel that I was put on this earth to do this, but I know that I need help to do it; your help."

We talked and talked for hours and then took a break, stretched our legs, and came back. The fire was lit the entire time. As I continued, I felt it even more. We had a connection, perhaps from some past life or another realm. Whatever it was, he felt it, too.

"We have to go through the spiritual leaders of the community," Mo said. "We need a grassroots movement in the communities through the spiritual leaders to do this."

Suddenly I could feel something coming. I looked up through the top of the teepee. A great gust of wind blew past us, ruffling the sides of the teepee and swooping down through the top opening. I felt a chill around me as the wind almost put out the fire's flames. We were the only ones that saw it. We both looked up to the sky and then at each other. This incredible wind had swept around us like a stampede of horses, and then it—and they—were gone. I could feel the energy of our horse ancestors in this place. It was confirmation for us both.

"We're going to have a ceremony tonight," Mo said. "Yuwipi (healing)."

It was now late afternoon. Mo announced that we would have a sweat. There was no way that I would do the sweat lodge with him. I was afraid I wouldn't have the stamina to take it and might interrupt the process, so I opted to sit it out. It was probably a good call.

Mo and his friends spent hours in the sweat. Joan, Dana, and I sat in lawn chairs and stared up at the Kansas skies. It was quiet at Mo's ranch, but also lively. Neighbors descended upon the property as ducks and geese ran after them. I reached into my grocery stash and had a granola bar. It was nice and peaceful at Mo's. Life was good here.

When Mo was finally done, we were invited into his garage, along with his neighbors and family, for a healing ceremony. There were more blankets and bearskin rugs covering the floor. Everyone was taking seats. Mo pointed to a space close to where he would be sitting and motioned that was for us.

"Yuwipi, is also called the shaking tent ceremony. It is a traditional healing ceremony for the Lakota for either the physical or spiritual being or both," Mo announced.

Yuwipi is something you have to be invited to attend. It's sacred. Mo and his relatives and friends got the garage ready for the Yuwipi.

They pulled down the garage door and got up on ladders to drill wooden planks over the windows. The room needed to be completely sealed so that no light got in for the ceremony. They were sealing every hole in the place.

"Today, we have special guests in from New York," Mo motioned to the four of us. "And we will be calling out to the animal spirits, in particular, the horse spirits."

Everyone was packed into the garage. The doors were closed, and the light was still on. Mo's friends and neighbors were on ladders drilling wooden planks over the windows. In one way, it scared me that I was going to be closed in this garage with all of these people. In another way, it was crazy exciting that we were here and going to be a part of this ancient tradition, still practiced in modern times. Was I reliving my past? I was nervous, anxious, excited, and curiously at home with it all.

The prep time seemed to take forever, as Mo laid out sage, fabrics, ropes, and other colorful things for this ceremony. He looked as though he was already going into another realm as they transformed the garage into a sacred space.

Finally, it was time to begin. Because I was invited to be there, and it was a sacred ceremony, I cannot share too many details about what was happening, but I can tell you about me. The room fell silent, and things started with drumming and song.

Kola hoye wayin kta ca namah'un yelo.
Kola hoye wayin kta ca namah'un yelo...

As the rhythm and chant got louder and louder, I could feel sweat trickle down the back of my neck. The air was heavy. It was stifling inside the garage already, and the atmosphere was getting intense. All of a sudden, the drumming, Mo, and another young man's voice seemed to crescendo and all at once before the lights went out with a poof, and there was dead silence.

My heart skipped a beat, and I jumped, feeling nervous and afraid. It was so dark, a black from another place. I blinked hard, trying to find any available light, but saw nothing. I opened and closed my eyes again as lights seemed to dart across the garage ceiling above me. Was

I seeing this, or was it all in my mind? I sat focused on my breathing and finally allowed myself to go with the energy of the moment, just to let go.

Mo started again chanting and praying in Lakota. The garage door-way rattled, and the walls of the house shook. On two occasions, Mo shouted out, "Manda, tell the spirits why you are here."

I wasn't sure if I opened my mouth to speak if anything would come out, but it did. I asked the spirit ancestors for help for the horses. On several occasions, it felt like something breezed by me, and once my hair even moved from a gust or what I thought felt like a feather across the top of my head. Then it seemed as if someone was painting a scene with horses on the wall behind me; those ledger-horse and native paintings. There was singing and chanting for a long time. Mo's young nephew had a beautiful voice and did most of the singing.

The lights came back on, and I blinked hard again. Mo, who was now seated in a chair, looked exhausted.

"Oh my God," I said to Dana, squeezing her hands. As I looked down, I saw the small bundle of sage in my hand that Mo had passed out to everyone at the beginning of the ceremony. I knew I had to keep this with me forever. Just then, the garage door began to noisily open, and we got up from our crossed legged positions on the floor. Mo remained seated.

I wasn't sure if I should approach him or not. I was unsure what the proper protocol might be. I left him alone and waited for every-one else to depart, trying not to be awkward about it. Mo finally got up from the chair and approached me. He seemed exhausted.

"Manda, what did you hear from the horses?"

I did have a vision during the ceremony, which I was waiting to tell Mo. I have had this intuitive psychic thing going on for most of my life. "Mo, you're going to get a present. The horse spirit has a present for you and wants to send you a horse. It's going to be a grayish roan horse," I said. Mo looked at me incredulously. "And we will work to-gether," I said. Knowing it would be true.

By the time we left, it was nearly 2:00 in the morning. I was so ex-hausted; I wasn't sure I was even in my body. I felt like I was floating around somewhere in the ethos. As we were leaving, Mo turned to me and said, "My Lakota name means He Who Catches the Horse." There was nothing else that needed to be said.

I felt I'd made real progress on the trip back from Kansas, but I wanted to meet with Mo again to get to know him better and keep talking about our future alignment for the horses. He and Sara Ann flew to New York that next month to spend time with me at the farm. Jon joined us, too. We talked strategy and how we could collaborate to help the horses and native people. We spent time eating, laughing, and hearing about his work on movies, films, and life in Los Angeles versus Kansas.

Mo promised Sara Ann that if she came to New York, he'd take her to see Times Square. She'd only ever wanted to see Times Square. We drove into the city and made sure to arrive after dark so that Sara Ann could see the lights and billboards in full effect.

I parked the car in a garage just two blocks from 42nd St—the heart of it all—and we walked over. Everyone was really excited, including me, as I love sharing and having people enjoy my hometown and a city that I love. Even if Times Square isn't my favorite, it is what people know about New York.

On one of the side streets, we were walking past a cigar shop, and outside stood one of those old carved wooden statues, the cigar store Indian. Jon pointed to it, and he and Mo decided to take a photo in front of it, one on each side.

Oh my god. That's a cultural appropriation from the 19th century, I thought. I felt so, so terrible for them because that's what they live with all the time.

"Here it's 2015, and that's standing out here," I said.

"It's the same thing for the wild horses," Mo said. "They are remnants of the past that have been discarded."

Jon gave the Cigar Store Indian the bird, and we moved along back to the car. We drove back to Long Island in silence. 1010 Wins gave us reports on the traffic, and I tried to avoid the gridlock along with any awkward conversation. Sometimes the truth is just too hard to live with.

At the end of the two days, Mo said he'd help. He'd work on helping me find land. We were setting out on the journey.

I connected Mo with Frank Kuntz, who runs the Nakota Horse Conservancy, dedicated to preserving a unique breed of horses that have roamed Theodore Roosevelt National Park and the Little Missouri National Grasslands for over a century. The Nakota horses are thought by many to be Sitting Bull's band. When Sitting Bull surrendered at Fort Laramie, they had to surrender their horses, an Indian's most prized possession. Many of the horses were slaughtered by the cavalry, but some did manage to get away.

Sitting Bull is Mo's mentor in every way. He's also a distant relative. When Sitting Bull was young, Mo's great-great-uncle was Sitting Bull's mentor.

I arranged for Mo to go out and see them and meet Frank. He didn't know about these horses, and it was a natural fit. It was a life-changing experience for Mo to be there with his horse relatives.

A few months later, Frank called Mo and told him he had a present for him. Frank gifted him a grayish roan Nakota horse.

I like to say that God has a great sense of humor, dropping an old Indian spirit into a blond, Jewish woman living on Long Island. Who else could get the job done?

9. IT TAKES A VILLAGE—OR A CONGRESSMAN

"Great things in business are never done by one person; they're done by
a team of people."
~Steve Jobs

I was starting to form my team. I knew, as I know now, that success is only possible with a great team. My mission was a big one, and I needed to compile the best people from diverse backgrounds to make it work. Following one more trip to see Mo—this time in Los Angeles, where he was performing as Sitting Bull in a play—he came on board officially with Cana. I had already been working on another key player, Congressman Steve Israel.

If you want to get anything done in Washington DC, you have to have a strategy, and that normally involves working with insiders.

Congressman Israel had not only been a US Representative since 2001; he had voted to protect free-roaming horses and burros in the West and was known to be an animal advocate. President Bill Clinton once was quoted saying, "Congressman Israel is one of the most thoughtful Members of Congress." It also helped that he was representing my home state of New York's 3rd congressional district, Nassau County, my county on Long Island.

In the summer of 2014, when I originally met Steve at the Hampton Classic Horse Show ASPCA panel event on horse slaughter, he and I were speaking alongside Georgina Bloomberg, local politicians, and horse rescues. One of the largest outdoor horse shows in North America, the Hampton Classic, has been going on for over four decades. It's not only a draw for top riders, who compete for hundreds of thousands of dollars in cash prizes but for the who's who of the New York area. You'll find top executives, hedge fund billionaires, reality show stars, celebrities, politicians, wealthy housewives & househusbands, all milling about the acres of show grounds.

The panel was held in a tent just off one of the main Classic shopping zones, where high-end boutiques sell big-brimmed straw sunhats, paintings by local artists, colorful blankets, on-trend bags, jewelry, scarves, trinkets, and more. You can come to the Classic and outfit yourself along with your Hamptons home.

Most people were shopping and spectating in one of their VIP tents during our panel, but maybe one hundred dedicated people attended. Those that did either wanted to learn about the issue of horse slaughter or wanted to meet one of the influential panelists.

In typical Hamptons style, there was champagne and cocktail mixer following the panel. A mad scurry to get in front of whomever you want to meet had already started during our wrap up. Ladies skillfully fixed their hats and reached under their chairs to grab their purses so that when the audience started clapping, they were poised to pounce from their lairs to take down their delegate of choice.

I didn't even get the chance to snag one of the champagne flutes dancing by on a waiter's round tray before I was bombarded by Nancy Mansfiel. I knew Nancy from high school. Her daughter was close to my age and also rode every year at the Classic, as did my daughter, and often me. Nancy always made it a point to seek me out at this horse show and try to find out the latest in my life with Albert. I swear she must have crushed hard on him when she knew him in her younger

years. Albert normally only attended the Classic once or twice during its eight days, and that was to see my daughter ride.

"Oh, Manda, you look amazing! I just love your belt and bracelet," Nancy cooed as she lifted up my arm to examine the large silver Native American bracelet on my wrist. She eyed my diamond rings like a Diamond District jeweler.

"Thank you," I oozed out, summoning every ounce of authenticity and grace I could muster.

Nancy was always hard to wriggle away from once you were entangled. Rats, she'd gotten me again! I gave a few sideways glances to see if the Congressman was still here. He was someone who I really wanted to meet. I noticed he had a line of people waiting to talk with him, and one of his staffers was hovering about, checking her watch with nervous regularity. Steve's ten minutes at this post-event were probably about up.

"Well, I just wanted to check in to see how life is going. I heard Albert had won another building deal. Isn't he so amazing," she grabbed my hand a little too enthusiastically, likely trying to get my full attention, which was clearly wandering.

"Yes, we're always so proud of Albert, our children, and I," I half smiled, emphasizing to Nancy that I did have children with Albert, and she'd best step off! "He definitely stays busy. That reminds me, I've got to catch someone, Nancy, so pleased to see you." She nearly tore off my wedding band as I fought to slip from her clutches. "I wonder if my jagged wedding ring drew blood," I smiled to myself as I purposefully strode over to Congressman Israel, decisively snatching a much-desired glass of bubbly without skipping a beat.

His staffer was already pushing back the crowds and announcing the Congressman had to depart when I caught Steve's eye. I horned my way around a woman in a large polka dot dress and noticed with surprise that Steve appeared to be making his way towards me, too.

In my most charming voice, "Congressman Israel," extending my hand, which he received enthusiastically with a smile. "Manda Kalimian, Cana Foundation."

"Manda," Steve smiled, exuding charm and good vibes. "What a great presentation. Your work sounds very interesting, must keep you busy."

I smiled back.

Steve Israel has this way of speaking with you that makes you feel like you're the only one in the room, even in a crowded tent at a horse show.

"I'm working on a plan to rewild America's wild horses on Native American lands, and I'm hoping we can schedule some time outside of this venue to discuss it."

"Wow! That actually sounds really interesting. Sure." Steve turned to his staffer and introduced me immediately. "Make an appointment for Manda to come and see me."

The short, pale blonde woman in her twenties with very thick-rimmed glasses, as were popular at the time, handed me a card and told me to call her on Monday.

Well, I called on Monday, and the next Monday, and every Monday, in fact, for some weeks before I could get an appointment. It just so happened that the appointment wasn't for his office on Long Island. That just wasn't available. I'd have to meet him in Washington, DC, at his office on Capitol Hill. I, naturally, took the meeting at whatever time he had free.

I was excited like a giddy schoolgirl to be heading to Washington for my first legitimate Capitol Hill meeting. I'd been to the Capitol building for other meetings, parties, and events, but this one was specifically to talk about my business and work for Cana, and it was for a major issue.

Because this first meeting was one in which I knew I had to make the best impression, I went shopping. It was a big deal to get a meeting with a Congressman. I knew I had to look the part.

I was pretty casual in my life. I ran my foundation from home and otherwise was a mom; I didn't go to an office. I didn't have suits or even wear many blazers. In true me fashion, I waited until the last minute to figure out an outfit. We were at a horse show in Saugerties, NY, the weekend before my trip to DC, so I had to hit the Nordstrom there. I walked in and told the first salesman I saw that I was headed to Washington for meetings and needed slacks and a shirt. He was young enough that I knew the word slacks was already dating me. This meant he was heading straight for the mom-jeans-&-more section, but that was okay with me.

He pulled out several dated options. I furrowed my nose and ended up going with what I thought looked the most in style and yet also conservative; a pair of gray suit pants with a slight flare at the bottom and a white designer shirt. I love scarves, so I opted for a knit black and white shawl. It was the end of the summer, so the wooly shawl was a little warm, but I figured I'd stick it in my purse while outside and then wear it indoors where everything was over AC'd.

My assistant, Dana, and I had spent hours working on a presentation. She was going to read it over again and put the final touches on it before the morning. I laid out my outfit the night before and had everything timed out perfectly for the morning commute. We'd be hopping a LIRR train to Penn Station, where we'd then get on the Amtrak Acela to arrive in DC an hour ahead of our meeting. Since Capitol Hill was just a few blocks from DC's Union Station, we'd just walk or cab over to the Rayburn House Office Building, home to Steve Israel's prestigious office. I'd heard Rayburn was a maze and knew we'd have to go through security, so had allotted some extra time for us in DC.

Apparently, not enough for Dana. In her early 20's and a recent graduate, this was Dana's first job out of college, and I made the mistake of becoming a little more friendly than perhaps a boss should be. Dana had started to treat me more like a mom or BFF than boss. I didn't mind most of the time. She was cute, smart, and understood me and the mission. Today, she was late for our very first train from Long Island to Penn Station, which could have a disastrous ricochet effect. If we missed our train from Penn Station to DC, we'd for sure be late. Trains left Penn Station for DC frequently, but the Acela, the fast train, was only every three hours. If we missed it, we'd have to opt for the next regional, which would only get us to DC with about thirty minutes to spare. And that was if it was on time.

I was pacing back and forth hysterically on the train platform, wondering if I should hop on and take a seat or not. I'd called and texted Dana, and she said she was five minutes away. The train was leaving in ten. I decided to hop on. I had to make sure one of us made it to DC on time. What was I going to do, call and tell the Congressman that I was running late? I'd never get a second appointment. I felt in my heart, too, that this meeting was meant to be.

The train was just about to depart as I saw Dana pop out of the stairs and sprint along the platform, her wide eyes peering into the windows to try to find me. I got up from my seat and leaned over two other seats to knock on the glass and get her attention. She wiped her hand across her forehead dramatically with a smile and then appeared again in an instant inside my train car.

Dana was average height and very thin with long, dark brown hair & eyes, thick eyebrows, and olive-colored skin. She always appeared neat and organized, even when she had been out until 4 a.m. with friends at a bar, as she apparently had the night before. Wearing tight cropped pants, black kitten heels, a black & white top, and a black blazer, she at least looked put together as she whipped down the aisle.

"Sorry. So, it was Jasmine's birthday at Long Duck's last night, slash, this morning. Eek!"

She crashed down into the seat beside me, smelling of a mix of espresso-laced Starbucks confection, spearmint gum, and a hint of tequila shots. I took a deep breath, wondering how to address this. I didn't want to upset Dana as I'd learned that my criticisms could sometimes lead her into a spiral that did more harm than good. She never really listened or learned from them anyway, so it was usually best to just let it roll, even though my blood pressure was currently through the roof, and I'd already sweated through my white and black designer button-down.

"I just have to finish a few things on the presentation." She set her large iced Starbucket on the floor and flipped open her Apple laptop.

"It's not done?" I gasped. "Dana, it needed to be printed!"

"Not to worry. It's almost there, and I found a Kinkos on the way to the Capitol," Dana smiled and rested her hand on my arm. "It's all good."

I turned my head and looked out the window, my heart beginning to race. Trees and houses ticked by quicker and quicker. We were already moving, and I hadn't even realized it. Dana had truly gotten on in the nick of time.

I hated going to Kinkos. They always messed your order up, and it always took forever. I could feel the anxiety creeping up with my temperature as I took off my shawl, fanning myself with my hands as we started the first leg of our journey into Manhattan.

Thankfully, we made the train to DC. After a cab ride, the usual drama at Kinkos, and an uber to the Capitol, we'd gotten through security and were click-clacking our heels down the windowless hallways of the Rayburn Building. I felt ant-like amid the large and spacious 1960's style corridors lined with big wooden doors flanked by flags every few feet. Each door had an American flag and the flag of that representative's state or community. Plaques announced the name of the Congressman burrowed away inside.

"The more senior you are in Congress, the better your real estate is." Dana recited as we hurried down the hall. I hated to be stressed, and being potentially late made me anxious. "Junior Congressmen get the basement dungeon-like spaces, while those who have been around for a few terms, rise up physically within the building to offices with impressive and iconic views of the Lincoln Memorial and beyond; that was Steve Israel's view."

Dana may not have prepared our presentation, but she got us to the gig, so, like Elsa, I 'Let It Go.'

We stopped to take a selfie in front of Rayburn as a commemoration of our first official congressional visit. After the hassle of standing in line and relentlessly fighting through security, we were finally in. We were click-clacking away, something I don't do too often. I was super impressed with the magnitude of the building—which takes up the better part of a city block—and we hadn't even reached the Congressman's office yet. We waited a beat to further collect ourselves before entering Israel's office and letting the staffers know we were there. We were actually five minutes early, so I powdered my forehead and checked my lip gloss. A good gloss is key.

Inside sat two large mahogany desks, one on each side of the room. I recognized one of the staffers from the Hampton Classic.

"Hi Breanna," I said with a smile.

"Mrs. Kalimian," Breanna rose up from her desk and walked over to shake my hand. I introduced Dana, and Breanna told us that it would be just five minutes, and we'd be speaking with Congressman Israel. We sat down on a leather couch and stared at memorabilia from his district in Long Island; photos with important and newsworthy constituents, awards & plaques from initiatives he'd worked on. It was his congressional life.

A few minutes later, and we were being led in. The Congressman greeted us with a large smile and a welcoming energy as he walked around from his vast desk to shake our hands.

Steve's light, bright, and giant office had a formal seating area, which he pointed towards, and we again sat down together on the big leather couch. Steve and Breanna sat in opposite upholstery-covered armchairs, a coffee table between us. Photos of Steve with President Obama and Heads of State, his wife & children, and memories from international trips lined the walls. One of Steve's passions is books and writing—as I would later find out—which explained the impressively stocked cases.

I opened with my, thank you for having us and got right down to business with my rewilding pitch, taxpayer savings, native lands, the benefits, upsides, and socio-economic opportunities related to emancipating wild horses from BLM holding pens and releasing them onto native lands. In effect, rewilding. I closed with why we wanted the Bureau to take part or at least give up some of the horses they were holding hostage. It also came over me at that moment that, by doing all this, we could actually make the Bureau look good, change their narrative, and their reputation as far as wild horses went; all the more reason to work with us.

Steve listened graciously, as I'm sure a good politician does and then smiled. But this smile I could see was real. I could see that he saw real merit in what I was saying. One of the Congressman's specialties was strategic planning; his wheels were turning.

"So, where have you done this; where can we see it?"

"Well," I took my time in answering, "Nowhere. I have been working on all the planning, but I need your help. I need to get to the Bureau of Land Management and the Bureau of Indian Affairs for land."

In Washington, I'd come to learn; there are so many things to fight for. Each Congressperson has their area of special interest and issues their constituents are expecting them to work for. If an issue or idea seems too complicated and getting other reps to sign on will be tough, it ain't happenin', baby! So, finding Congressman Israel, who was a Long Island representative and an advocate for wild horses, was almost a dream come true for me. I was a constituent and had an issue in an area that was of interest to him. I had struck gold! He was intrigued and said that we should meet again. "This time on Long Island," he smiled as we exited his office, back into the main waiting area, where two staffers made sure we left as quickly as possible.

Some months on, Dana and I had made another trip to DC where Steve introduced us to three other congressional leaders that he wanted us to pitch on rewilding. They were representatives from Arizona, Minnesota, and Kentucky. He even made time to have lunch with us and his staffer that trip to discuss possible Indian reservations that might be interested. I was thrilled. Things seemed to be happening.

By the time spring came along, it was a perfect time to invite Steve to the farm to see the horses and to meet Mo. Since he had offices on Long Island, I extended an invite to him to come to my farm for lunch. It was a beautiful midsummer's day, and I was pleasantly surprised that Albert joined as well; I knew I was doing something right.

Mo and Steve clicked right away. I, of course, kept track of the fifty minutes we had until Steve had to leave while taming the food and directing the conversation. Mo is a beautiful orator. When speaking about his culture and horses, he is the most passionate and hypnotic speaker. He spoke to Steve about his background, horses, Native Reservations, and our plan. Steve was engrossed the whole while.

Our moment ended when Steve's staffer interrupted with, "We have to leave in ten minutes, Congressman."

That was when Mo looked down at the ground and picked up a small white pebble. He explained to Steve that in his world, even the smallest rock was a relative and had meaning and reason for being. Mo looked Steve in the face and said, "Please join us on our mission to save the horse nation." With an outstretched arm, Mo handed Steve the little white pebble.

Steve took the small pebble from Mo and put it in his pocket. He then looked Mo in the face and said, "I'm in. You had me at hello."

Steve enthusiastically shook Mo's hand. They gave each other one of those pats-on-the-back that guys give other guys, and we ran to take some pictures all together as Steve's staffer worked to rush him out to their next meeting. It was a grand day indeed!

The world of politics had been as foreign to me as speaking Japanese. It wasn't a world that I ever thought I would enter, and yet, here I was with a VIP pass. This was a giant leap for one girl.

I went to the city in August to attend an event that Steve hosted in which the alternative medicine expert and meditation pioneer, Deepak Chopra, also attended. The Congressman and I worked together to organize a screening on Capitol Hill for a film called Running Wild, a documentary about the life of Dayton Hyde, a conservationist who ran a horse sanctuary in South Dakota's Black Hills for many years. Hyde was an animal advocate who really made a difference for wild horses. With this kind of event, you get mostly staffers, many of whom attend for the free wine and food, but the point is that they will learn something about your issue and take that back to their congressman or congresswoman to at least get your cause noticed.

I learned on these various trips that, to get things done, you have to make friends and allies. Washington, for sure, wasn't an 'I' location. On the political front, you had to team up with politicos and influencers on both sides of the aisle.

I also learned that when you get meetings with these politicians, the first thing you always ask is, how much time do I have, because it could be ten minutes, twelve minutes, or twenty minutes. Or it could be two. Most of the time they'd tell me, "You have fifteen minutes." This means you really have to get your elevator pitch down in specific sound bites that will leave an impression.

Outside of DC, we worked to make a difference, too. I organized several of the Hooves on First events at CitiField. These were big fundraisers, and every year I'd try to make a splash, even bringing in live Mustang horses one year. Another year, it was the cast, including lifesized horse puppet, Joey, from Broadway's War Horse musical. Congressman Israel would always take the time to attend.

In the fall of 2016, at a meeting in his Long Island office with Mo and me, Steve let us know that he wasn't going to run for reelection. He was set to retire by the end of 2016. He had been canvassing for

Hillary Clinton, flying all over. I could see in his eyes he was tired. It was time. But then a wave of panic came over me. Who could I find to help my rewilding mission for the wild horses when Steve left DC? Nobody would be like Steve Israel.

Over the next few days, I was consumed with what to do and how to keep the work going with Steve's help. I had an idea. I invited him to the farm to talk. It was at that meeting that he and I had a frank talk about what he was embarking on after Washington and where Cana could fit in. He told me he was creating the Institute of Global Affairs at Long Island University and doing some consulting for a handful of people. I asked him if Cana could be one of those people; I offered him riding lessons on his now favorite horse of mine and office space in the barn, anything he wanted. He was going to think about it and let me know. He called me 20 minutes later and said, "Let's give it a try for six months." I was extremely grateful and relieved.

The Congressman became Cana Foundation's strategic advisor. With his guidance and advice, things really started to move in Washington. As I said, it takes a team or a village of experts. Insiders really help. With Steve's new role, I would soon have Congresswoman Nita Lowey out to the farm for dinner. Senator 'Heidi' Heitkamp, Congressman Adam Schiff, Tom Suozzi, and Peter King. Democratic Congresswoman Betty McCollum from Minnesota also visited. She's like a sister to Steve, and they've done a lot of work together in DC. She participated in our legislative panel at the Hampton Classic, along with Congressman Peter King.

After spending some time working with Mo and me, Steve recommended I bring on an Executive Director for Cana to help me organize better from within. I brought on Lauren Corcoran-Doolin, as our executive director. Lauren worked for Hillary Clinton's campaign. She was the number one political organizer on Long Island at the time. Steve helped to find her. Lauren knew everyone and had been in and around politics her whole life. We were in good hands.

Steve recommended we set up a Political Action Committee. Ours would be billed as Saddle PAC. They're a way to raise and deploy money to get officials elected or perhaps defeated. You put money into a PAC because you believe in what the PAC is supporting, and that money helps support the campaigns of the people that will work to press forward those initiatives as part of their congressional or senatorial platforms.

Lauren would help me figure out how to raise money and fully utilize the Saddle PAC. It basically consisted of Lauren sitting by me and taking notes as I phoned friends and strangers to ask for money for the PAC. It was exhausting. You have to be a certain kind of person to keep asking for money and taking all the rejection. Lauren could see this wasn't my strong suit, but anything for the horses, right?

In reality, this was what all politicians had to do all of the time; sit in a booth and have call time, smiling and dialing for dollars. My location is primarily Republican, so raising money for a PAC that is supporting horses and the environment with Democratic candidates is no walk in the park.

We organized a PAC event at my farm for Democratic Congressman Adam Schiff, which was a highlight. Our PAC would also help support Deb Haaland, a Native American Democrat from New Mexico running for Congress, and Sharice Davids, the first openly LGBT Native American from Kansas. Both of these women believed in supporting wild horses and the environment. These ladies won their elections and were the first American Indian women voted into Congress. Congresswoman Haaland has since gone on to become secretary of the interior. We were quite proud to be a part of that history. It was a sort of roundabout way to help us further our cause of bettering the treatment of America's wild horses, their habitats, and the lives of indigenous peoples.

Though we did a lot of good, the whole PAC project was a further eye-opener for me on US politics. I wondered how any politician ever got anything done in their jobs because so much time was spent fundraising. Half of the time that a politician is in office, they're running around raising money to get reelected. A congressional term is only two years. They're already lobbying for reelection during year one, and year two is just awash with campaigning. Everything is dependent on money, which is not only wrong, it's absurd!

The most disheartening part of it all was the challenge of changing perceptions. I was coming around to seeing that more and more every year. Everybody's truth is based on an agenda, and many times, this agenda is personal; I'd even venture to say, selfish. Even if something is true out in the world and bad things are happening, if it's not touching someone personally, why should they care. People's truth is based on the agenda they want to see and how that affects them financially.

I'd make some small ripples of change, but to effectuate real change, would almost take an act of God. It would be a hard and long fight.

While we were winding down our PAC days in the fall of 2018, we had a bigger issue with which to contend. The government was trying once again to make horse slaughter plants legal in this country. This would be a cheap and easy way to dispose of all the wild horses in government holding pens and put horse meat on your supermarket shelves and restaurants. The government would do this by appropriating funding for USDA government inspectors who would inspect horse slaughter plants. You see, without a USDA stamp on your meat, you cannot have a slaughter plant to sell meat.

Over 85% of Americans do not believe horses should be slaughtered for meat; it is un-American. But, for reasons revolving around oil, fracking, and agricultural farming on public rangelands, certain Legislators keep trying to bring horse slaughter back despite the position of the American people. Do you want to worry about having horse meat in your hamburger?

At one of our bi-weekly meetings with Steve, we were brainstorming how to help or what role Cana could have in DC to say "No" to horse slaughter. This was when Steve suggested something we don't normally do. He thought that we should align with the other horse advocacy groups and take out an ad in Politico.

Politico is one of the most influential political publications, read by members of Congress, lobbyists, the media, and beyond. As complicated as the wild horse issue is, it is equally as complicated trying to work with wild horse advocacy groups. I have always made it a practice to stay in my own lane and do my own thing, but, with Steve's guidance, a large group of horse advocates was able to come together with Cana to say "No" to horse slaughter.

Steve designed the ad and drafted the language while Dana and I organized the groups. I collected whatever funding each group could offer. It wasn't about the money for the ad as much as it was the energy of the moment that carried the day.

We got a full-page ad with nearly thirty wild horse advocacy groups aligned together. That was a first, and Congress was forced to stop and listen. I believe with our combined outreach efforts and Steve's help; we were instrumental in stopping the slaughter bill from passing that year.

Out of all the things the Congressman and I have done and tried to do, the accomplishment that I am most proud of is the language that Steve would help us get written into the FY2020 Interior Appropriations Budget Bill. Everything seems to work in layers. Building layers of accomplishments and credibility in DC and the rest of the world.

Steve had talked about getting language for rewilding as a viable management tool for wild horses for some time. It was a dream to think it was possible until one evening in May when Steve called me with some news. He couldn't see that on the other end of the phone, tears were streaming down my face as I heard him utter the words. "Our rewilding language made it into the Appropriations Budget Bill."

I had to take a moment and compose myself before I could answer him. I couldn't thank him enough. My admiration for him at that moment was immeasurable. These two sentences tucked away in a huge piece of legislation would perhaps one day change the course of everything.

There was no money appropriated to the language, but it didn't matter. For the first time in US history, 'rewilding' is written into legislation, and it is connected to helping free our wild horses, a new way to manage our horses and give them a better life while helping save lands and environments. I am so proud to have brought this message forward. The next step would be to have the BLM utilize this amendment, and part of their yearly funding would be allocated to this initiative, but one step at a time, I told myself.

You must always believe that anything is possible—because it is.

10. MORNING JOE

If you don't like the news, go out and make some of your own.
~Wes Nisker

I 'm running around now with this beautiful actor, a Lakota spiritual leader, and a spokesperson for his people. What better person to have with you on a morning TV show? Mo became the spokesperson for Cana. Once we started working together, I kind of felt like Mo's agent.

I scored a big coup getting us a spot on MSNBC's Morning Joe. I'm a big believer that if you put positive energy out into the universe, you get it back. I'm not saying that you should do positive things only be-cause you want to get something back. You should do the right things for the right reasons. When you do things because they are good and they are the right thing to do, you'll be paid in dividends.

My farrier, Tommy, had been working with my horses for years. I know him well and also have gotten to know his wife Dina and their three children. They were all riders, too. Dina rode dressage and had a Grand Prix level dressage horse named Dulce. Grand Prix is the top of the line when it comes to dressage horses. Dressage is a little like ballet on horseback. Dina rode a lot, and she loved this horse; she had him since he was three years old. He was like her child. She'd broken Dulce and trained him, but with three kids now, household finances were tight.

Tommy and I had a heart-to-heart one day. He really wanted me to take Dina's horse for a while because they really couldn't afford the up-keep. They had him leased out to a little girl, but the horse was nearly 17 years old and unhappy. The situation was not working out for either of them. She also couldn't afford to lease him anymore.

I really didn't want to feed or keep another horse at this point, but I knew they were in a bind, and I felt for Dulce and Dina. I told Tommy to bring him to my stables, and I'd take care of him for a while.

Dulce came to my stables, and I tried to ride him a bit, but I could feel he was unhappy. I was not a dressage rider, nor was I his person. He seemed to be suffering from a sore back. I wasn't overweight or doing anything too crazy, but I am intuitive to the point of being psychic, especially when it comes to animals. I knew what had changed.

The next time Tommy came by to work with my horses, I had another talk with him. He was shoeing a horse in the hallway of my stables when I stopped him between hammer hits.

"Tommy, I need to talk to you about Dulce. He's not happy without Dina. He's Dina's horse. He's devastated without her. She's had him forever, and now for the first time in his life, he's at some strange barn with strange people and a strange child riding him for the last six months. He's a nervous wreck. He's skin and bones. He doesn't want me. He wants Dina."

Tommy let go of the horse's hoof, and the horse set it on the floor. He looked up at me. I continued.

"I will keep the horse here, but Dina's going to have to come to ride her horse because he's going to die without her. He's going to die of a broken heart."

Tommy smiled and nodded his head, trying to pretend that this wasn't making him extremely happy because it would make Dina happy.

"Manda, I appreciate you telling me this because Dina's been so depressed without Dulce, but I'll make you a deal that I'll shoe two of your horses for free and also shoe Dulce, of course, in exchange for keeping him here longer. And Dina will be so happy."

Not paying Tommy for two horses being shod each month barely covered the horses' shavings, hay, and the drama of it all, but I did it for him and for Dina.

Dina would visit a few times a week, and I came to see a change in Dulce from day one. He was more like a dog than a horse. This was a huge horse, and he was so sweet and gentle. Dina would put her five-year-old daughter on him, and he'd strut around. He put on weight and thrived.

After a few months passed, I figured Dulce was finally settling into his new home here at the farm. We offer a very Zen environment here, but things weren't great for Dina. As a nurse practitioner, Dina was finding it hard to juggle work, the kids, and Dulce. She asked if a friend of hers who worked in New York City might be able to come out to ride once in a while. I didn't like too many people coming to the farm that I didn't know, but since she was a friend of Dina's, I said it was fine.

I became friendly with Dina's friend, Bridget, who happened to be German and a beautiful dressage rider. She started to come twice a week, including on the weekends with her husband, Mike, and their rescue dog. Her dog loved hanging out with my dog pack. At the time, I still had seven German Shorthaired Pointers, Willy, Midge, New Year, Hadley, Brian, Peanut, and Elliot. They and the horses really ruled my property and my life, but when you have sixteen acres on Long Island, the more, the merrier.

One thing led to another, and I found out that Bridget's husband Mike had gotten a new job at MSNBC, doing all of the web work on the Morning Joe with Mika Brzezinski. It was actually Bridgett who knew and understood what I was doing with the foundation. She worked for an animal rescue on the side and was very empathetic to the plight of the wild horses. She suggested we approach Mike about how I might get a story on Morning Joe.

We all sat down together in the office at the farm, and I shared in detail what was happening with the horses and what Cana was doing to help. Mike was very supportive and thought Mika would be interested in the story as it had a political message. Mike went to bat and pitched our story with Cana and me as experts on wild horses and the politics surrounding them. It was November of 2017, and there was a key vote by the Senate Appropriations Committee on the horizon that could reopen the door to allow horse slaughter in the United States. My foundation had run an anti-slaughter campaign that included billboards in Times Square, New York. We also organized the formation of a coalition of animal, environmental, and health organizations from New York called New Yorkers Against Horse Slaughter. We organized a nationwide unification of pro-horse organizations to put pressure on key committee members.

Dangerous language had been covertly inserted into the US House's massive spending bill that put over 80,000 healthy wild horses at risk for slaughter. The last line of defense was working to ensure that the Senate didn't allow this dangerous language to become part of Trump's appropriations bill when the Senate and House went into conference. So, I got the gig! Mo and I were going to get interviewed on MSNBC to talk about the politics surrounding this upcoming vote and why anyone should care about horses and horse slaughter. I was over the moon about going on MSNBC. It was huge publicity for Cana and our cause. I remember when I called Steve to tell him, even he was shocked. He had been an MSNBC contributor and knew Mika and Joe well. It was a busy time for Steve, but we got on the phone, and he ran through some quick pointers on what to say, how to say it, and what not to do. All I could think about when he was talking was how am I going to remember all of these things, so I didn't remember most of what he was telling me.

After that call, I thought about the fact that doing the right thing for Dina and her horse generated the opportunity to go on television. How else would I have met Bridget and Mike? Again, when you do things for the right reason from your core, these are things that come back to you. The right thing for the right reason, I always say. I felt like it was Dulce's way of saying thank you, so, based on this, I felt sure we would do just fine.

Mo flew in from Kansas the day before Morning Joe near the end of October 2017. We had to be there at 9 a.m., but in order to get into the city by then, we'd have to leave at 7 a.m. from Long Island. That meant that Mo had to have his braids done and be ready on time. Praying and braiding is a sacred task and takes time.

I relied on Mo to carry the spiritual part of our journey, to keep us connected to the great creator on our mission to save the horse nation. Now that we needed help getting to the train and the NBC studios on time, I was doing the praying for that.

I picked up Mo from his hotel at 6 a.m. and headed for the train. Dana was with us, and Steve had arranged for Harrison, his press staffer, to meet us at NBC to make sure we got upstairs, and all went well. He and Dana were in charge.

We'd be taking the good old LIRR to Penn station again and then to the subway to get to the iconic Rockefeller Center, where NBC was housed. Mo had never been on the subway, and I hadn't been on the subway since I was a shop-girl at Bloomingdales when I was 22. Though New Yorkers normally pretend not to notice unusual people or things on the train, I noticed a few people giving Mo second glances. The three of us made for an interesting trio.

Mo was wearing a black felt cowboy hat along with a black button-down vest, red button-down shirt, colorful bandana assembled like a necktie, jeans, cowboy boots, and dangling feather earrings, along with his signature long black braids. I was in a black turtleneck with the big feather necklace that I always wore—and pearl earrings. My long blonde hair was blown out to perfection, and I was rocking cowboy boots. Dana, well, she was always looking cute as a button.

As we got out of the subway and walked to the entrance that said NBC Studios, there was Harrison waving to us. He was hard to miss, but then again, so were we. He and Dana conferred, and in we went. We got our badges at the security desk, and Harrison escorted us up to the 4th floor. There was a young woman waiting for us, and she escorted us to what is known as the green room. We plopped down on the little red couches, took our coats off, and caught a breath. OMG, we'd made it! I was actually in the NBC studios going to be interviewed by Mika Brezinski for Morning Joe. This was crazy. How I manage to make things happen, I just don't know, but I seem to have a knack for it. Intention is a powerful force.

I always like to do my own makeup when heading to appearances, even if I know there's going to be a makeup artist. They sometimes can make you look like a different person, and I prefer, for instance, subtle glossy lips and a more natural look. Mo and I went back and forth practicing reciting facts and figures related to the number of horses out on public rangeland and still in holding pens. I wanted to make sure that we were both clear and ready when the lights went on, and it was go-time.

In my mind, I thought that Mo would be much more ready and prepared than me. He's an actor who memorizes scripts and recites them on camera for a living. He's not afraid of cameras. Though I give the occasional speech for my foundation and regularly mix and mingle with people, I don't normally do live television. Needless to say, I was a little nervous.

They pulled me into the makeup room. I was out within a few minutes, following the makeup woman telling me I looked pretty good to go and dousing me with a bit of clear powder to take away any shine. Mo received the same treatment.

Back in the green room, we were watching other interviews being conducted in the main studio, and I was psyched. I paced around the room a bit to get out any nervous energy. I was ready for this. The universe had sent me here, and I was ready!

A producer in her 20s wearing a headset and carrying a clipboard knocked and then came in to greet us. She was casually dressed in jeans and a bright green sweater with high top pink sneakers. She explained that before the interview, there would be a video clip with some background on our work and the foundation.

"They edited it from the footage you provided. Next, Mika will lead into her questions. Okay." She uttered the word okay really slowly, not looking like she really wanted questions or a response.

"Okay," I said back slowly.

She let out a sigh, smiled, and left. We'd just made her job easy.

My heart started to race a bit as we were finally led upstairs to the Morning Joe studio. Whenever you do a morning show, whether it's live or not, everyone seems to be in a rush. Of course, time is money with a whole production crew, equipment, well-paid hosts, and important guests.

Another producer ushered us into the well-lit studio, past a photographer configuring a large camera on wheels. There were thick wires leading up to cameras, various equipment on the floor, and a team of people buzzing about. The producer sat me down at one end of a large glass table under the lights with Rockefeller Center as the background on a glass wall. Mo sat to my left, and they placed Morning Joe coffee cups in front of us, giving us the option for coffee or water. I realized that I was parched and opted for water.

Mika entered next and introduced herself with a swift handshake. She wore a V-neck dark navy-blue dress, accenting her tan skin, cropped blonde hair, and a dazzling smile. I was a little star-struck. She sat down beside Mo and talked to a producer in her earpiece while I took another gulp of water and realized that I needed to sip because I was almost out.

The young producer was back and must have realized this was the case because she swooped over with a glass pitcher of water and refilled my cup immediately. She, too, talked with someone in her ear. I looked over at Mo, who seemed to be transfixed by the scene around him, his eyes glazed over as he fidgeted with his scarf. I knew he was used to being on set, having worked on films like The Revenant, The American West, and Cowboys & Aliens, to name a few, but he looked a little nervous.

The other two hosts then entered the room, Mike Barnicle and one other nice man that was co-hosting. But they were in their grey and navy suits and ties, looking very proper and political. They sat on the far side of the table beside Mika, checked their notes quickly, and then, they too were talking to producers and each other, mumbling about the earlier morning guests.

Morning Joe is all about news and political topics, so one of our main headlines today would deal with how Trump's budget would impact wild horses.

"Manda and Mo, thanks so much for coming today," Mika said, looking over at us with a pro smile as she shuffled around some papers with notes and then immediately went back to talking in her earpiece. "We don't often cover topics related to horses, which I love, so I'm excited for this one."

"Yes, my daughter competes in dressage," Mike piped in.

Before I knew it, we were at three, two, one, and the green lights on the cameras flashed on. We were rolling. Looking back at the video from our filming online, I was so focused on me at the time that I didn't notice at the beginning Mo fidgeting with his bandana tie, looking almost nervous as Mika started us off.

"Manda, tell us more about the goals of the Cana Foundation. This is about horses."

I gave a quick smile and started in. I knew once I got started, I would be okay. That's what I told myself anyway.

"Thank you, Mika. Yeah. Cana Foundation has created a rewilding movement through horses, humans, and habitat. We believe that America's greatest asset is the wild horse. It's an interesting concept," I noticed the camera focus in on me and sat up a little straighter, "because most people do not understand what's happening to wild horses and what's happening to the wild horse is happening to our public rangelands, and it's happening to all of the American people."

I kept trying to think back to my call with Steve and his media training tips and advice. He had told me to remember to keep smiling. When in doubt, smile, and make sure to answer their questions with short, concise answers that are to the point. If they ask something, you don't want to answer, just respond with something you wanted to get across in the interview and don't fidget. I tend to use my hands to express myself, so I was nearly sitting on them to keep them from going all over the place.

Mika came back with another comment and question, "And you're looking at legislation right now that is being passed, but also Trump's budget and what it means for horse slaughter?"

"Exactly," I countered. "We are looking right now at the Omnibus Bill, and we want everybody out there to contact their senators and tell them that horse slaughter is not acceptable. They are trying to enact to make horse slaughter legal in this country to help eradicate their wild horse issue and crisis."

I sat back for a second, glancing over at Mo. His eyes were like saucers. He looked like he was frozen in a trance. I gave him a kick under the table, and he sprung to life managing to get in some of the key points we'd discussed, including that tens of millions of acres available to horses have been lost since the 1970s.

"If you look back to 1971, there were 43 million acres available for wild horses, and since then, the numbers have dropped down to 28 million and not only have they lost their roaming rights, but they have to share that 28 million acres with cattle with whom they're outnumbered 50 to 1. As a Native American, I know the trauma and the devastation that occurs when your ability to roam has been reduced," Mo continued.

I wasn't surprised by the next comment by Mike, who had never heard of horse slaughter and said he only really knew about horses from watching movies. This was not uncommon in our modern, urban lifestyles.

Mo went on to explain about horse roundups on our public lands, his voice fumbling a bit as he tried to clarify for the hosts the scope of the issue.

"Mika," I said, looking directly at her, "They chase them down with helicopters. They separate the families. They bring them into holding facilities. These horses sit in holding facilities all throughout the West, costing us, the taxpayer, between eighty and 100 million dollars each year to keep those horses there, while public rangelands are leased out to special interest groups for cattle ranching."

Mika seemed to be on board and wanted to know how people could help. I responded and directed people to go to our website so they could find the contact information for their senator and reach out.

"Horses have walked the journey with man since the beginning of time," I said, getting pretty passionate at this point. "We may not be here today if it wasn't for the horse."

It was my closing statement, and it was so true. Mika and Mike thanked us for coming, and we were ushered out quickly. Dana and Harrison were waiting for us. I could see Harrison was already on the phone with Steve telling him we were done and that he thought that we did a good job. In other words, there were no catastrophes. I couldn't wait to get Dana aside and ask her what she thought. She knew what I expected of myself.

The next guests were already coming in for their close up. It was a whirlwind, as we stepped outside into Rockefeller Center to the sounds of people chatting, taxis honking, and general Manhattan mayhem. Harrison bid us farewell and rushed off to meet Steve; I gave Mo a big hug. I felt like I'd just won the presidency. Mo just seemed relieved that it was over. He loosened his tie and cocked his hat back slightly as we stood in front of the Atlas statue to take our post-interview photos. We decided on lunch at Limani, an upscale Greek Mediterranean restaurant at Rock Center, where I decided to have a glass of wine with my halibut. It was a good day!

Later that day, back home, we kept checking to see if the segment was put up on the MSNBC website. Wow! To see yourself is so different than you imagine, but I must say all-in-all, for my first time, I didn't suck.

I got to speak with Steve Israel, who saw the segment. He was proud and supportive. He said we would go over it in detail at our next meeting.

When we did meet, Steve was a bit more candid, pointing out some of our mistakes. We had some good laughs about it. You have to laugh at yourself and not take it all too seriously. You do the best you can, but the important thing is to keep doing it,

It did make me think about Mo's future live TV experiences and my own. I felt more confident in what I could accomplish when put to the test. With a few more coaching segments, maybe I could do more of this TV thing.

Steve surmised that the segment was going to be very useful in reaching elected officials, many of whom tuned in to Morning Joe, as well as people who could help to affect change. He said he'd email the link around, too, to make sure it was seen by the right eyeballs.

In the horse advocacy world, it was a big deal that somebody got network coverage for the issue. We'd just accomplished something huge. It was just one of the many ways I was trying to work smartly to bring our goals to fruition. I was taking on Washington from DC, NYC, and beyond and I was feeling up to the task, ready for whatever was coming my way. Please scan the QR code to see the video of the appearance.

11. CAMBRIDGE

Life was given to us a billion years ago. What have we done with it?
~Scarlett Johansson from the film, Lucy

Who knew that my next step would be to take the Manda and Mo show international? The Cambridge Conservation Forum was having a Rewilding Symposium, the first of its kind. The program was to be held in January of 2019 in the David Attenborough Building at Cambridge University. It would bring together the top conservationists, landowners, farmers, stakeholders, scientists, ecologists, economists, and thought leaders in a public forum; a prestigious event from all perspectives.

Dana was always very good at scanning the internet for current information on the who's who in horses and rewilding. One day she sent me an email with a link to the Cambridge Conservation Forum. It looked amazing. My wheels started turning.

The next day I mentioned to her that we should definitely try to go to Cambridge for the event. I was thinking, "How fun and cool to just go, listen, learn, and network, network, network!" I started to look up airfares out of curiosity and Dana said; "You know the submission date for speakers closes in 2 weeks."

In that moment you could hear a pin drop. I looked at her, she looked at me. "What do you think?" I cautiously asked. I thought we should go to learn and connect, but never did I think we would be of the caliber to present.

"I think you will get in." Dana excitedly stated.

"Really? What the hell! Go ahead let's fill out the application."

The thought that I would be accepted to speak at Cambridge amongst all of the Harvard, Yale, and Cambridge scientists and organizations was crazy. But, it didn't hurt to try. I thought to myself, "If by some miracle I get in, then I'll worry about what to do." I always likened myself to Scarlett O'Hara in Gone with the Wind. She always said, "After all, tomorrow is another day." And so, it would be.

We submitted to present "Rewilding and Its Effects on Nature and People," focused on rewilding Wild Horses and efforts in the USA. The presentation would include our efforts to get rewilding instituted at a local and federal level, but more importantly, we would discuss the situation here in the States for the wild horses and our government, roundups, slaughter, and what Cana's ideas are for helping through Rewilding initiatives. I had no idea if they would take me as a speaker. I'm not a formal public speaker, nor have I had any real speaker training. I never really worry about these things though. I always believe I will figure it out, teach myself, or make it work, I have to. I had recently been on TV, so I thought I'd give it a try. Intuitively, I knew I had a better chance with Mo on the agenda. He brought a completely different perspective to England; one that was necessary.

The actual term 'rewilding' was only coined in recent decades, and its definition has changed over time. With rewilding, plants or animals are reintroduced into an environment in order to restore and grant more balance to ecosystems. The end goal is to make an environment livable for even more plants and species that may have once roamed there.

For America's wild horses, which are so connected to many of our Western lands, placing them back on the lands where they once roamed has a variety of ecological and economic benefits. Wild horses are considered natural stabilizers. A clear link has been established between wild horse populations in forest areas and the carbon sequestration potential of that ecosystem. Horses are grazers. They help with grassland management and encourage biodiversity. Like birds, horses also disperse seeds. On the economic side, releasing horses from BLM holding pens would save taxpayers tens of millions of dollars as well as offering socio-economic opportunities to communities. Plus, who doesn't believe that we're all happier when animals are living better lives?

In Europe, rewilding is more of a well-instituted concept and practice than it is in the United States. The charity, Rewild Britain, whose aim is to rewild five percent of the entire country by 2100, actively works on partnerships and initiatives to reintroduce species and rewild areas of England, Scotland, and Wales. Across England, beavers have been reintroduced; in some places this has been met with controversy. Nevertheless, the industrious beavers have had a positive effect on many areas where they've now built their homes, especially in flood prone locations, where their lodging helps to reduce area flooding.

There are various destinations where conservationists are testing rewilding; some, travelers can even visit. In West Sussex, the turtle dove, nightingale, and cuckoo species that had disappeared from the UK, have been reintroduced to a rewilding estate and are thriving, along with other biodiverse plants and species.

A big proponent of these initiatives, who helped launch the rewilding movement, would be presenting at the Cambridge conference. George Monbiot, the famed UK environmentalist and writer, was posing a question with his talk. "Could rewilding restore not only the natural world, but also humanity's prospects of getting through the century?" Having devoted a lifetime to speaking out about the environment and what's good in the world in general, Monbiot also penned a book on rewilding in 2013 called, Feral, Searching for Enchantment on the Frontiers of Rewilding. I would have considered attending the conference just for the chance to see George speak and perhaps to meet him even briefly.

It was fitting that the conference was being held in the UK at Cambridge, where rewilding has become such a hot topic in recent years. In the United States, rewilding was happening, too, though the term itself wasn't always used to describe it. The American Prairie Foundation in Montana had been working to create the largest nature reserve in the US. They reintroduced bison to their lands in 2005. Bison help control grass heights and their reintroduction has brought new birdlife to the prairies. At the American Prairie Reserve, tourism, too, is being implemented to help create new jobs along with a renewed appreciation among people for nature and the environment. Travelers are invited to visit the reserve and go horseback riding, hiking, biking, hunting, geocaching, and camp out or stay in huts and safari lodges; bringing new jobs and an economic boost to Montana.

In 1995, wolves were reintroduced to Yellowstone National Park after being absent for more than 70 years. The wolves killed off some of the overpopulated deer, but also altered their behavior. The deer came to realize that if they didn't want to get killed by wolves, they should avoid those places where they'd be most vulnerable to attack, like the valleys and gorges where getting trapped was all too easy. Those places, without deer to nibble away, began to regrow with grasses, taller trees, songbirds, beavers, otters, muskrats, ducks, ravens, bald eagles, and various reptiles and amphibians. Like putting the right parts in an engine, everything starts to work again and get into balance. George Monbiot had narrated a short documentary about this rewilding project in 2013, which would go on to be watched by over 40 million people on YouTube.

I hadn't wanted to tell anyone about our submission in case we were rejected, but I was already forming in my mind what I might say if I were asked to speak at the illustrious conservation forum in Cambridge. No one ever died from daydreaming, did they?

Then, on the morning of November 19th, 2018, I woke up, reached for my phone as we all do every morning, and there it was, an email from the CCF. I fumbled for my glasses so I could read the email that began with:

Hi Manda,

Thanks for sending us your proposal to talk at the CCF conference on Rewilding and its effects on nature and people. We're excited to say that we would be delighted to have you present on day 2 of the conference. We have allocated a 20min session for you, along with 5mins Q&A, followed by 5mins for people to move between sessions and rooms; so, 30mins in total.

The email went on to give a number of instructions, but, in that moment, there was no reason to read any further, OMG I have been admitted and invited to Cambridge to speak on behalf of America's wild horses! Leaping out of bed, I started screaming and doing the happy dance around the bedroom with the dogs. Singing the, 'I am going to Cambridge' song. You know the one, I'm sure. I had to keep pinching myself to see that I wasn't dreaming. All I kept thinking was, "Wait until I tell Congressman Israel. He won't believe it."

I was over the moon. I knew this would be a turning point for me professionally, but also that I'd learn so much from the members of academia, scholars, and also real world rewilders who were attending. I ran to email Steve. He was as impressed as I had anticipated. We were expanding our sphere of influence.

After much planning, practicing and organizing, it was January 8th and we were getting ready to leave. I must have packed and unpacked several times in preparation for the trip. It was a big deal. Mo was especially nervous, having never traveled abroad and feeling the pressure of representing his people, the Lakota nation, in the UK. Albert was so proud and impressed he was honored to join us. Being a seasoned traveler, Albert had one small neatly packed bag. Dana and I had huge suitcases with an assortment of outfits.

We all got to the airport and had a bite to eat before boarding our night flight, which would be uneventful. We used points to upgrade to business class and the vegetarian meal on British Airways wasn't half bad. I downed a glass of Champagne and was able to sleep an hour or two before we landed at bustling Heathrow. Since Albert was joining us, he treated the Cana crew to a car service straight to Cambridge. Otherwise, on Cana's budget, we would be taking a car to King's Cross and then the hour-long train ride to reach Cambridge.

I sat looking out the window at the verdant English countryside as we drove to Cambridge. I just couldn't believe we were here. Cana, arriving to Cambridge for the Conservation Forum. Who would believe it?

Even thinking about Cambridge made me feel slightly smarter, and as our classic black cab approached our lodging, I took a deep breath, closed my eyes, and smiled. We'd made it!

I was reveling wearing my long brown suede coat as Mo helped me out of the cab onto the cobblestone driveway of the Edwardian style University Arms hotel in the center of town. A crisp breeze ripped around the pillars of the neoclassical portico. I yanked up my blue woolen scarf and buttoned up. Even though it was cloudy, I donned my sunglasses. The driver unloaded our luggage and a bellhop dressed in a red coat and pants loaded our things onto a luggage cart. Was Cambridge ready for Cana and our message? More importantly, was I ready for Cambridge?

I felt like I was on the set of a movie. Just down Regent Street, the spires of a gothic church rose above three story red brick and sandstone buildings. Students and professors whizzed by boutiques, a bookstore, and cafes on bicycles. As the large green doors of the hotel opened, we entered the stunning, capacious lobby to the smell of geraniums. My high boots clapping on the black and white tiles and a greeter ran over to start explaining our location.

"We're situated right on Regent Street against Parker's Piece, a large park and one of many green spaces where locals and travelers might laze on down to read a book, play football on the weekends, or walk their dogs." He spoke rather quickly with his heavy British accent and slight lisp. In his gray wool jacket and red tie, the pale thin man with thick-rimmed glasses looked like a professor himself so he fit right in. "Cambridge is a dog lover's paradise, so if you like dogs, you'll be right at home."

The man smiled and I smiled back, turning to look over at Mo, who was mesmerized by the black and white photos of students rowing on the River Cam which lined the walls of Hotel du Vin, one of Cambridge's charming hotels, located in an old University building. I noticed that the hotel concierge seemed to be side eyeing Mo. Though the Hotel du Vin had all manner of celebrities passing through, it wasn't so often that a Lakota leader from America visited. Mo had on his beige cowboy hat, dark Levi's jeans, large silver belt, aqua button-down shirt, and a black wool suit jacket.

It was close to lunchtime and we'd arrived a day before the conference started, so that we could acclimatize—as they say in Britain—with Cambridge and, of course, do a little sightseeing. We decided to freshen up and meet downstairs to refuel in the hotel's bistro before hitting the town. While Dana told me, she'd need a thirty-minute power nap and shower, I knew that after a quick shower, I'd be ready to go. I was beyond excited to be there.

I love it when hotels go the extra mile for guests. A handwritten note along with fresh fruit, chocolate, and a bottle of red wine were laid out on the desk of my suite, which overlooked bustling Trumpington St with its many stone historic buildings and cobblestone streets.

I decided to leave a soak in the posh clawfoot bathtub for a post presentation celebration and took a longer than expected steaming shower, before quickly organizing my cross-body travel purse for a day outdoors.

Albert is a seasoned traveler and, as he is in real estate, has an affinity for architecture. He had already looked ahead at some locations of interest, and I had already earmarked a few musts for this trip: see Trinity College, designed by Sir Christopher Wren, stroll along The Backs—the rear grounds of Cambridge along the River Cam, soak in the Gothic English architecture at King College Chapel, have a pint in a pub, grab tea in Market Square, get a photo beside the Bridge of Sighs, meet as many experts as possible, network to the fullest during the conservation conference, give a kick-ass presentation, and meet George Monbiot. An ambitious agenda for my three days in Cambridge.

Our main focus would be at the all-important conference, so this afternoon was the time to pack in the sightseeing. After lunch, Mo decided to stay in and get over his jet lag, having traveled the furthest of us all coming from Kansas to NYC, to London, to Cambridge. I completely understood, but also felt that Mo seemed a bit tentative in his skin at Cambridge. Super confident in his home community but, understandably, Mo was a bit overwhelmed by this trip. I knew that he felt pressure. He was representing his history, ancestry, and people in another nation. He was going to be speaking the living language of his people in a presentation at Cambridge University. A first for both Mo and the conservation forum. We had already opened the door to change. I hoped a good nap and night's rest would set him right.

Dana and I almost opted to bike around for the afternoon. The hotel had these super cute bright blue bikes available but decided to go it by foot. Cars are discouraged around Cambridge, but taxis abound, and many people use cycling as their primary mode of transportation.

The David Attenborough Building is not in walking distance from the hotel, but nearly everything is, it just depends how long a walk you want to take. We decided to head off in that direction so as to be sure of where tomorrow's symposium would start, and to make sure we knew where everything was located. My stomach was a bit in butterflies as we passed the Museum of Archaeology and Anthropology on the University of Cambridge's stately campus. The second-oldest university in the English-speaking world, its prestige has been solidified over the centuries with notable alumni including Charles Darwin, John Maynard Keynes, Sir Isaac Newton, Jane Goodall, Virginia Woolf, and Steven Hawking. Those who like to read relish in the fact that the university has over 100 libraries housing millions of books, including every book ever published in the UK or Ireland.

Thought by many to be a national treasure in Great Britain and whose voice and works have inspired millions with visions and information on the natural world, David Attenborough's name marks the large modern building where the Cambridge Conservation Forum would be held. Today this building is home to Cambridge's Museum of Zoology. We snapped a photo outside, and I took a beat to say a brief thanks to the universe for getting me to this point.

"Wow. I can't believe I'm going to be speaking at Cambridge tomorrow." I squeezed Dana's hand and we both did a short happy dance. Perhaps I'll place a video of said happy dances on the Cana website at the appropriate time.

Albert was focused on experiencing the famous choir of Kings College, as we took a walk along the Backs to find The Bridge of Sighs, a covered bridge at St John's College, prominent in many movies and TV shows. The rest of the afternoon was mostly spent getting lost amid historic colleges, popping into the occasional shop or church, and truly getting a feel for the vibe of this beautiful, rich city.

The Forum was two days and the first day was lectures and introductions in the cavernous David Attenborough building. I was only too happy that we were presenting on the second day. I needed to get the lay of the land and find my groove. It was good for Mo and me to be able to sit and listen to others to feel sure we had everything that we needed for our own presentation.

After a good breakfast, we all walked over to the Hall with determination. There was excitement, but a calm across the group. Albert and Mo always kept a brisk pace and Dana and I were running to keep up on the uneven cobblestone sidewalks and roads. As we stood outside the building, we took a group photo of all 4 of us about to enter the David Attenborough building. It is still hard for me now to conceive of how far we have come from that first trip ten years ago to the rescue in the Hamptons.

The David Attenborough building is not only home to the Museum of Zoology, but also the Cambridge Conservation Initiative, where around 150 academics teach and conduct research on topics related to the environment and natural world. With a grand, light-filled atrium as its center, the building was designed to reflect this. One entire side of this open space is comprised of a four-story wall of plants and vegetation. Just walking in and staring up the greenery to the glass ceiling—even during a cold winter day—was a breath of fresh air.

When we entered, we were greeted by a team of young people that were running the forum. Actually, they knew who we were from the moment we walked in and I was greeted by my name. Four Yanks in Cambridge; we stood out. Everyone attending and working there made a huge fuss over us for the fact that we came all the way from America to attend. It was lovely, as they say in England. As opposed to, "It was awesome" as we say on Long Island. We were celebrities before we even did anything.

We had great seats, front and center, and the program was prodigious. I was so glad that Albert had opted to join us. It turned out to be a great learning curve for him and gave me huge credibility and back up to my ideas and goals with him. I often feel like he must think my creativity gets the better of me with my ideas and concepts, but here we were sitting in a room filled with people that are all likeminded and treating Mo and I like celebrities. It was a good and cathartic thing.

The next day, I woke up before sunrise. I knew I wouldn't be able to sleep in so I made tea and decided to take in a Cambridge sunrise. I wanted to run through our presentation one more time, before donning my Navajo-made black and white duster sweater, black turtleneck, and pants; getting ready to take on Cambridge.

Mo met me for breakfast at 7 a.m. in the downstairs bistro, a large room lined with wooden floors and wooden tables whose walls were covered in colorful art of all shapes and sizes. Sketches of Cambridge's gothic cathedrals, colorful vintage posters of men out rowing, paintings of mallard ducks, classic old bicycles, and cars gave a feeling that we were dining in one of the university's halls instead of a historic hotel. I ordered the works: eggs, sticky buns, pastries, and another cup of staunchly steeped tea. I noticed that Mo wasn't as famished, but then he had spent the afternoon and evening napping, while I walked the entirety of Cambridge.

I freshened up in my room and changed into my presentation outfit, a chic black dress and high black boots, plus some of the jewelry I'd purchased from a woman named Crystal Davis in Telluride, Colorado. She had been a schoolteacher on the Rez for native children and had amassed quite a collection of jewelry and art, but that's a story for another time.

Once I was dressed and ready to go, I sat myself down in the big easy chair in the corner of the room. I closed my eyes and took some long deep breathes. From the depths of my heart, I thanked the powers that be for getting us here and asked for help to make sure that I spoke with eloquence and represented the horses honorably. I then stood myself up, took one last look in the mirror, and off I went, full of confidence and purpose.

Our presentation wasn't until the afternoon, but we had a few sessions we planned to attend that morning. I was focused on a seminar by Rewilding Europe and the founder, Franz Scheppes, was speaking. Australian feminist writer and academic Germaine Greer, who has rewilded a small forest in Essex, England, opened the conference to a packed auditorium. Veterinarian and Royal Veterinary College director, Camilla Benfield, spoke about some rewilding pitfalls related to parasites and disease. Harold Stone of Rewilding News presented the various definitions and interpretations of rewilding, including lifestyle rewilding, something I was keen to hear more about. Prerna Bindra, a wildlife conservationist and author, addressed rewilding in India. It was truly a global conference.

The modern lecture room in which we were to speak, seated around 120 people. The presentation options were online, and you were supposed to sign up for presentations that you were planning to attend. I had been following our attendance throughout the week to see how many people were coming. My biggest fear was that we'd travel all the way to England, and no one would come to hear us speak. As the days drew closer, I'd come to see that our slot was completely full. One less thing to worry about. We were at our room a half hour early to sound-check and make sure the run-of-show was tight. Already, a few people were trickling in to take their seats; a good sign.

"So, Manda, this is it. Cambridge University," Mo said mellifluously with a smile, placing his arm around me as Dana snapped photos of us up by the podium emblazoned with the Cambridge Conservation Initiative logo. Albert was hunkering down in the front row, organizing himself to film our presentation. I suspected he was more nervous for us than we were.

Mo seemed like he was getting into the zone. I'd gotten to see him prior to taking the stage to perform in LA and, there too, he was super focused. He always did well in front of an audience. I, on the other hand, wasn't as practiced, but was psyching myself up for it.

Before we knew it, all the seats were filled, and a staffer shut the door and motioned to us that it was time to begin. They had given me a mic, dangerous, I thought. It was large and cumbersome, and I was a newbie at this. I fumbled around for a second, put the mic down and asked if everyone could hear me. With my hands free to express myself, I led off the presentation, explaining what Cana Foundation is and why we felt compelled to speak at the Cambridge Conservation Forum. We showed a short video about wild horses in America and what our foundation believed should be done, before I started my speech.

"I don't know how many of you are familiar with the plight of the wild horse, back in the Americas."

I looked out and didn't get too many nods, so figured I was dealing with an audience unaware of the struggles.

"We gave you a short briefing of what's happening. Our government does not recognize our wild horses as indigenous to the Americas. So, the wild horses that are free roaming on our public range lands are considered Mustangs. They consider these the horses that the Conquistadors brought over originally. We know otherwise. We understand and believe that the horse is indigenous to the Americas and has been there for over 10,000 years. But because of this misconception, or manipulation, this is the way the government manages these formerly wild horses. They chase them down with helicopters, round them up, as you've seen from the video, and imprison them in government holding facilities. We currently have over 70,000 horses in holding facilities while ~50,000 are still free roaming."

I was moving back and forth in the front of the room, attempting to make eye contact with the many Brits, but also Aussies in the audience. It was a hard room to read, potentially not as facially expressive as an American audience, but I felt like they were listening really well. The slide presentation was on a large screen behind me and I would glance up at the screen and back at my notes. Dana was standing at the podium to my left and when I finished talking about the subject matter on each slide, I would pause, and she would know to change the slide to the next. Once I got rolling, it didn't seem so hard, as I was engrossed in my subject matter and in-the-flow.

I continued. "This is the issue. The government is using our public range lands for private interest; oil drilling, fracking, corporate farming, etc. The cattle lobby has the lock on most of the land and the cattle that they farm are exported to China. So, the horses really have lost their habitats and their lands. This is what we are facing at this time. They are caught in the crossfire between the special interest groups and the 1971 Wild Horse and Burro Act that ties them to the lands, but no one really wants or abides by the act. They are trapped without a place to really call home."

I explained further about the plight of the wild horse and how rewilding them back on the lands of Native American communities could be beneficial to horses and people. "Native communities have lands and horses are of tremendous cultural and spiritual importance to native peoples. If we could trade off land on reservations for these horses in exchange for infrastructure, education, or something that the tribe needed, that would be a win for all.

"We must move past just the science of rewilding and move into the connective piece (and also connective peace). It is indigenous teachings of connections to the planet and the horse that will help us to understand this connection energetically and spiritually. Having said that, it would be my greatest honor to introduce my partner, and empowered Native American of the Lakota, Moses Brings Plenty."

The audience gave a rousing round of applause and Mo took the microphone, greeting the people in his native language, Lakota, and it is a beautiful language to listen to.

"The horses gave us dances, and an understanding of how to live in a community. When we speak about horses, they are at the forefront of our cultural identity. They are at the forefront of our lives. For many years my people have lived their lives on the back of a horse, and there's no greater teacher."

Mo spoke so beautifully. I could tell that he was really connecting with the audience and had found his inherent peace to communicate at the next level. They were mesmerized by him, tall, handsome, and charismatic, but more than that, he was offering them something they craved, a greater understanding of the relationship between man and nature. He was speaking the gospel and truth of his ancestors, here at Cambridge. "What a moment," I thought to myself as I stood to the side and watched in surreal disbelief. Sometimes it's the smallest accomplishments that give you the most satisfaction. I was inordinately proud of us.

Mo continued. "We are all descendants from a tribe from somewhere in this world. And it is crucial that we begin to understand there is no shame in looking back. Where did we come from? Who assisted us along the way?"

We'd exceeded our 120-seat capacity and were now standing-room-only as Mo continued his heartfelt dissertation. When he finished, he re-introduced me, and I joined him for the Q&A part of the program. Mo stepped to the side of the podium and I made some jokes about Mo having all the fun and I get to do all the dirty work, when Mo interrupted and said; "Excuse me folks, I have a special treat for you." I looked over at Mo, not quite sure of what was happening, but I knew it would be good.

He moved back to the front of the room and said, "I am going to sing you the ancient horse song of my people."

He picked up the mic and began to sing. His performance evoked tears. Everyone was moved and enthralled. Mo finished to a standing ovation, and I then continued, having been somewhat upstaged, with my Q and A. Mo can be a hard act to follow, but I don't mind. My job is always taking care of business. If only I could bust out a song that rocked the joint. We all have our strengths.

George Monbiot, who I had spotted in the back, must have slipped in during the middle of our presentation. I gave Dana a look and gestured with my eyes wide over to Monbiot, hoping she'd understand that we needed to try to catch him after. To make extra sure, I also shot her a quick, somewhat over-obsessive text. We were set to meet him shortly after our presentation. I wanted to make sure we knew exactly where, and be early.

Our Q and A went on for some time and, if I do say so myself, I excel at repartee with the audience. Can chat a bit. As people got up and were moving around the room and coming up to the podium to speak with us, Dana put on our music video, Run Free Tonight. The energy in the room was powerful. We made our mark at Cambridge; we delivered admirably.

Our timing would lead us from our lecture hall to a corner of the cafeteria, where sitting alone, on his phone, was George Monboit, waiting, as promised for a 15-minute meet and greet.

Monbiot's bio read like a global adventure novel. Canoeing for weeks across the central highlands of West Papua in the far east of Indonesia and eating insects to stay alive as he chased down a story about migrants and indigenous people for his first book—Poisoned Arrows—was just one of his harrowing life adventures. He'd lived all over the world, writing about the plight of people and the environment for his own books, in addition to stellar publications like the BBC and The Guardian. I'd seen so many of his talks and interviews that I was a bit starstruck, finally seeing him in person.

Wearing a burgundy V-neck merino wool sweater with a black t-shirt underneath, jeans, and brown, lace-up boots, he had the look of a modern British journalist. With glasses and slightly greyish, dark, messy hair and a bit of scruff on his face, he looked like an older Harry Potter, of sorts.

He greeted me with a friendly, "Well, hello Manda," as he looked up from gathering his coat and bag.

"George," I beamed, deciding not to call him Mr. Monbiot, even though George seemed so casual. "Yes, I'm so glad you were able to see some of my presentation."

"Fascinating and such a good idea," he said, gesturing for me to take a seat.

"Thank you! That means a lot coming from you," I smiled. I turned and introduced everyone else and we all sat down. Such as when we would meet with legislators who only had a very small window of time, that was how this was. I could feel a slight pressure from George as he was thinking of where he had to be next, but he was always polite. Dana and I grilled him with rewilding questions while talking about what Cana was doing. He was fascinated with what Mo had to say from the indigenous perspective and was extremely interested in using the horse as the architects of the land.

"Yes, yes; Hind gut grazers," George said, thinking out loud. I hadn't thought of it this way.

Hmmm. I thought to myself. Another feather in my cap for the day. It doesn't get better than this!

George politely excused himself after about twenty minutes. He was the keynote speaker closing the conservation forum later that day and had to finish preparing. We were all floating on air from the morning and ran out and into the heart of Cambridge for a quick bite and back to get our front-row seats for our new friend, George Monbiot, and his closing lecture on Rewilding; restoring not only the natural world, but also humanity's prospects of getting through the century."

As expected, he was incredible. He is a wonderful speaker and his British accent lends itself perfectly to his passion when he speaks. Somewhere around the middle of his talk, I thought I heard him say; "I met the people from the Cana foundation here from America, saving wild horses, they reminded me that wild horses are hind gut grazers and are important to building biodiversity in our ecosystems."

I turned to Dana, she looked at me. I looked at Mo and Albert, "did he just say Cana?" They all nodded back at me. Okay, well there it was, right here, right now, at the David Attenborough Hall, the name of my little Cana Foundation was referenced to 450 attendees by George Monbiot in his keynote address. We came. they saw, they heard, and we conquered! What can I say? Cana had gone global. Quietly, slowly, but definitely.

Albert needed a chain tether to keep me from floating out of my seat for the rest of the speech. It really couldn't get any better.

After two standing ovations and some thank you speeches up on the stage, the forum was over. We were all chatting with various people as everyone was leaving. Albert came over and whispered in my ear that we were all heading to the pub and gave me a wink, congratulating me on a job-well-done. It felt good. You know when you've been married to someone for over twenty years, sometimes it's one little thing that makes all the difference in the world; the wink of an eye, a hand on your arm as you exit a car, a hug when your child accomplishes something extraordinary, or something small. Albert's wink today meant something special.

It was just a few minutes' walk to The Eagle, a famous Cambridge pub in the city center and one that seemed quintessentially British. The old stone building stood out with its big red door and golden eagle emblazoned on the glass window above the entrance. Mismatching upholstered chairs and sofas were set around wooden tables in the dark restaurant and pub. The smell of strong English ale mixed with wild mushroom soup.

Dating back to 1667, The Eagle has been a watering spot for scientists from the University for decades. It's at The Eagle that Francis Crick and James Watson announced they'd, "found the secret of life" during a 1953 lunch. They had done something rather remarkable. They'd come up with the structure of DNA. During World War II, Royal Air Force pilots would frequent The Eagle, marking the occasion to drink there with lighters to the ceiling. Their names and historic graffiti are there for those who want to look up while having a pint today.

Always crowded with students and tourists, the pub had a heightened-buzz this evening with the additional conversation and energy of conservation conference attendees. Our group somehow got a large table, so we could all drink and digest what we'd just experienced. We ordered a variety of appetizers and all got pints of the local ale, including the so named, Eagle's DNA after the famous discovery.

English conservationist Helen Harwatt, who taught at Harvard and studied the role of livestock-reduction in helping to reduce climate change —and had spoken about rewilding's potential in curbing carbon—sat beside me.

"So, Manda," she said in a clipped British accent as she grabbed a chip—what we call a french-fry—from the basket on the table. She took one of the smallest bites of a fry I'd ever seen. "With all you learned about the rewilding work that England is doing, what can we learn from what you all are working on across the pond?"

I took a sip of my pint, thinking for a minute, looking at her shiny, sleek black hair. "The human energetic connection to the land. Placing back the animals and letting the grass grow and the trees thrive allows the land and environment to thrive, but when you add thought, prayer, and song to the mix, things thrive even more. I mean, you heard Mo sing. There's an undeniable energy that releases into the environment. Native Americans understand this."

Mo heard me speaking and chimed in as well.

"It's through ceremonies, prayer, and song. It's part of our connection to the land that we're rewilding. It connects us to the planet."

Helen smiled. "Well, I may have to have you both pay a visit to some of our projects in the countryside here or back in Boston. Absolutely beautiful and wild, but a spot where your energy could certainly do some good," Helen gave us a cheers and we all concurred, clinking our glasses of frothy, dark, fabulous ale.

It was the best way to end a successful day on my own campaign trail. I was so glad we'd come to Cambridge. What I'd already learned here was extraordinary and I was excited to be bringing it home to the USA.

We left Cambridge on top of the world; opening the Cambridge Independent newspaper on our ride back to London, only to see a photo of Mo and me as one of the highlights of the conference. On the way home, Mo was able to express the depth of emotion that he had in representing his people and the horse in England at the CCF. I didn't fully realize how deeply moved he was and how much it meant to him, on behalf of his relatives, that he was there. I was overwhelmed with joy for him and felt great satisfaction from knowing I was a part of something bigger than all of us.

Our chit-chat during the ride to the airport denoted how we not only survived, but that we left an impact. We had spoken to hundreds of people and re-educated them on the importance of the horse as a participant in rewilding and a keystone species, including the great George Monbiot.

Our confidence, following Cambridge, would drive us into the coming months in a push for changes to U.S. legislation related to horses and rewilding.

Amid all of this, Steve left Long Island University, where he was chairman of the Global Institute, to run the non-partisan Cornell University Institute of Politics and Global Affairs in New York City.

We decided to work together on a new project. We would hold a conference on horses and rewilding at the United Nations. It would be co-hosted by the United Nations Environment Programme, The Institute of Politics and Global Affairs at Cornell University, and Cana Foundation. We'd have legislators there to talk, along with Steve and me, and some experts we'd enlist. Steve had us working on a list of Global advisors that could speak, too.

I referenced earlier the FY2020 Interior Appropriations Budget Bill. It was in May that the language we had wanted inserted, got approved. The flow of events since we went to Cambridge were powerful and dynamic. We were on a roll. Rewilding language was now in the budget bill and we'd be discussing it at the UN conference. The universe couldn't have been any more cooperative in lending a hand to save our horses.

I know you have been waiting for it, so here's the language, as it reads in the bill:

> *"Rewilding. The Committee recognizes the value of horse rewilding as one of many herd management strategies and encourages the Bureau to explore collaborations with suitable organizations and willing landowners to adopt, transport, and locate horses to appropriate habitats at no cost to taxpayers."*

But still there was something missing. I kept pleading with the universe to send me some much-needed support. I constantly feel like I am on an island by myself with all of the responsibility to save the horses firmly on my shoulders. I needed help. I needed to feel someone else understood what I did and was loyal to the cause, someone who was like me. I did the right things, for the right reasons, and it would be nice to not always feel that I was alone in this way. I needed to have someone who had knowledge, power, and clout to help continue to move our message forward into action. This led me to the next part of my journey that was totally unexpected, a hallowed institution in New York City, a museum where children and adults long to spend the afternoon; and the night.

12. SERENDIPITY

"Nothing binds you except your thoughts; nothing limits you except your fear, and nothing controls you except your beliefs."

~Marianne Wilson

Most people don't realize how powerful they are and that the key to all things is manifesting. We are so powerful that we can actually manifest anything we want; our dreams, desires, wishes, goals, and future. We can create everything that we want. It just may not be exactly how we thought it would be.

Manifestation is the key to everything, and that is what keeps me going. Every day I manifest my future, and I keep putting out there what it is that I want. That's what gives me hope, and hope is what keeps you going. The hope of the future is what keeps me working and gives me the light and the path that guides me as I walk this journey. We are all just manifestations of our own device, as the Eagles say in their Hotel California song.

We don't really realize how powerful that is and how powerful we are. If we envision what it is and we envision where we want to go, and we see where we want to be, we can manifest and go and get whatever it is that we choose and what we want. It is the universe's greatest pleasure to help guide us to our goals.

It took me the better part of my journey to learn this. I've started knowing what it was that I want to do, and I have a clear vision of the end result and what that looks like, but I don't always know how to get there. I've made a lot of mistakes along the way and had some pitfalls, or rather fell into some ditches, but I keep seeing the end result, and that is when I've started to realize that I am actually creating the path to my end goal.

So, when my friend Elise told me about Dr. Ross MacPhee, the curator of the mammalogy department at the museum of natural history, I didn't realize how much more powerful I had become at manifesting the help I had long asked the universe for.

The world of wild horse advocacy is a whole world in itself. Everyone knows each other, and if you don't today, you will tomorrow. Elise Vaughn works for the governor of Colorado, running his labor department. She is also an advocate for the wild ones. She goes to Washington a number of times a year and volunteers for a handful of horse advocate groups imparting information about wild horses. Being inside the government, she knows how legislation works. Whenever she went to Washington, she'd try to meet with certain staffers for certain congressional leaders advocating wild horse legislation and bills.

I met Elise when I organized the advertising campaign with Politico back in 2017, spearheaded by Congressman Israel. I spoke about this earlier in the story. It was where we aligned ~25 wild horse advocate groups to help to hold the slaughter vote from being passed. It was working on this initiative that I got to know Elise and came to see that she was a kindred spirit.

Elise had been at a Porcine Zona Pellucida conference last summer. PZP is a vaccine-derived from slaughterhouse pig ovaries used to control wild horse populations on the range. It is hard to imagine creating a vaccine out of slaughtered pig ovaries and injecting that into another species, but that is the best that the 100's of millions of our federal tax dollars that have been invested into this program have produced thus far; All to further aid the continued pillaging of our public lands.

There, she listened to Dr. Ross MacPhee give his presentation on the horse as a native species to North America. After meeting him there, she believed we might have a synergy and that Ross—being a true proponent for the horse—may be helpful to furthering Cana's cause.

I looked him up only to find he was just in Manhattan at the American Museum of Natural History, a short train ride away. His title was a mouthful: Ph.D., Curator, & Professor of the Department of Mammalogy/Vertebrate Zoology & Gilder Graduate School. I was looking online at a somewhat dated and grainy black & white photograph of Dr. MacPhee at an archaeological site somewhere in the world, and although I can't explain it, there was a familiarity about him for me. I just knew that if I reached out to him, he would answer.

I sat down in the office of my stables, surrounded by the good vibes of all my horses, the faint smell of hay wafting through the air, and the peaceful sound of contented horses eating. It took almost an hour to craft what felt like the right first email. I was hoping he would respond to my invitation to attend an important UN event.

I have this funny little thing I like to do when sending off an important email. Before I hit send, I take a moment, close my eyes, and ask to make sure I get a little help in making whatever it is I need to happen, happen. Then I send my email along with all good vibes. I gave this one an extra moment or two to reaffirm. This was a biggie.

Dear Dr. MacPhee,

I would like to introduce myself; I am the founder of the Cana Foundation. Our goal is to bring rewilding initiatives using the wild horses and the understanding that wild horses are a native species to America. Elise Vaughan was in contact with you at the beginning of September about the Colorado 'native' wild horse bill and suggested I might reach out to you.

We recently achieved rewilding language in the FY2020 appropriations bill. I have attached the press release with the link to the bill for your review.

On April 15th, 2020, there will be a conference at the UN on rewilding, highlighting wild horses as a keystone species in rewilding. My organization has sponsored the Institute of Politics at Cornell University to help effectuate the conference, and now the UN's environmental program is a co-sponsor of the conference as well.

Born To Rewild

*I am located on Long Island and would love the opportunity to meet
with you about your work and possible participation in the UN event.*

I am looking forward to hearing back from you.

Manda Kalimian

I finally hit send, sitting back in my chair and feeling like I'd most
certainly accomplished something for the day. My hope was that I'd get
an answer in the next few days. I had it all planned out. If I didn't hear
from him in a day or two, I'd re-email him for a follow-up.

Just an hour later, I received an email response and was over the
moon. I did the Manda dance; you know the one. I ran past the stalls,
giving my horse, Cello, a pat, and ran back to my desk to reply. I wanted to respond right away while he was still potentially going through
email. I read his response.

Hi Manda,

*Thank you for your message. I am certainly willing to meet but am
distressed by the lack of any detectable coordination among wild
equine advocacy groups and therefore wonder what the point of the
UN conference would be in terms of useful outcomes.*

*As I am sure you know, I am on your side of the house scientifically,
in that I view Equus caballus as merely the domesticated version of
a species that has been around for the better part of 2 million years.
Ancient DNA shows that populations of this species on either side
of Beringia were still exchanging genes as recently as near the end
of the last ice age. Although it had the misfortune to die out in the
New World 10,000 years ago, the horse is a North American native
species by any reasonable biological standard.*

*I am prepared to speak to that, in any venue, but must leave the
politics of rewilding to others.*

Best wishes,

Ross

I bit my bottom lip as I thought about a good response. He did say he was willing to meet. The front door was open, and this time I didn't even have to try another way inside. It was all I needed.

Ross,

Thank you so much for your email. The conference will also reference thoughts about rewilding related to other animals. As I am the proponent specifically for the horses, it will be the first time that information about the wild horses can be brought to light in a different context.

There are a handful of advocates with whom I work. I had coordinated efforts with the larger group at various times when it was needed to help the horses, but for the most part, I have chosen to travel in my own lane for the last ten years, and they respect that. Elise Vaughan is on my advisory board, and I have the support of Ginger Kathrens when it comes to rewilding and a few others with whom I associate.

Please let me know what would be best for you to meet for a brief chat. Thank you again for your consideration, and I look forward to meeting you.

Manda

I hit send again, and this time didn't sit back in my chair. I needed to get some nervous energy out. I grabbed a bridle from the wall in my tack room and went to Cello's stall. I needed to take a ride and think.

Four days passed, and I hadn't gotten a reply from Dr. MacPhee. I was on pins and needles, hoping we'd get to meet. I just needed to get my foot in the door, but it was in these moments when I was hoping and praying for something good to happen that I would start to question myself about everything. Why was I doing what I was doing? Perhaps I was just not good enough, smart enough, or strong enough to effectuate enough change to make a difference for all these wild horses. I would look around at my horses, each one a rescue in one way or another, and there, somewhere deep in their soulful dark eyes, is where I would see the person that I am supposed to be, and so I'd fight on.

Finally, Ross sent me an email with some available dates, and I picked the first one, November 25th, 2019. I couldn't wait; I ran to call Elise and let her know.

The Museum of Natural History is located on the Upper West Side of Manhattan, on Central Park West right across the road from Central Park in the upper 70's. Spanning a few large city blocks with a planetarium, library, and over 40 exhibition halls, the museum's impressive architecture is a mix of Beaux-Arts, Romanesque, and High Victorian. It lies in Theodore Roosevelt Park, named after one of the museum's founders, Theodore Roosevelt, Sr. the father of President Theodore Roosevelt.

In the spring, the park surrounding the museum brims with colorful tulips and cherry blossom trees. Locals walk their dogs down the brick sidewalks, read novels, and eat ice cream on park benches. In the fall, the autumn leaves frame the imposing architecture, as school children get led in droves to the hallowed institution. Founded in 1869, the mission is: Discover, interpret, and disseminate—through scientific research and education—knowledge about human cultures, the natural world, and the universe. To visit is exciting. To be of the caliber to work here or, like Dr. MacPhee, run a department is beyond impressive.

On my November visit, the last of the fall leaves meandered through the air and crunched beneath my knee-high brown leather boots as I approached the 77th street pink granite castle entrance. The museum is massive, so it was a good thing that Ross had sent such deliberate instructions of where to meet. I had taken the train in from Long Island and planned to arrive early.

It was 9:35 a.m., and my meeting wasn't until 10 a.m., so I went across the street to the New York Historical Society. Not everyone knows about it, but they have a lovely café and bookstore. I ordered a hot Earl Grey tea and checked my phone again. Dr. MacPhee was running a half-hour late. I pondered going back to the Natural History Museum to explore an exhibit but decided instead to stay in the coffee shop and prep. I put on clear gloss and checked myself in my compact mirror to make sure I looked sufficiently academic. I didn't, but I'd have to do.

10:15 hit and I jumped up from my café table, gathered my coat, and went back across the street to the old castle entrance. Stepping inside, I felt that I was walking outside of myself. It's hard to explain, but I just knew that this meeting and this day was going to be important.

Down the stairs and through the glass doors to the security desk, I told the guard who I was meeting. He photographed me and gave me a sticker. I had some small banter with one of the two female security guards behind the desk because she liked my pocketbook. I was carrying my signature bag with the image of Audrey Hepburn on it. We all need a little Audrey.

"Dr. MacPhee will be right down to get you." The guard gave me a wink.

The minute I looked up and processed where I was, a rush of nostalgia came back to me. I was in the Grand Gallery entrance, where the 63-foot Great Canoe used to be suspended from the ceiling. I remembered it from childhood days spent at the museum. When I was a kid, we lived just a few blocks away on Central Park West, and we were always visiting the museum. It's so huge that you can't possibly see everything in one or two or even three visits and, since we lived so close, we'd pop over for any special exhibit or just because our housekeeper-slash-nanny, Jane, wanted to take us for a walk inside.

If you're from Manhattan, Queens, Long Island, or Brooklyn, the Museum of Natural History is everything. I grew up in the Dinosaur Hall, staring up at the four-foot-long jaw of the T-Rex, wading through crowds alongside fossilized dinosaur footprints and millions of years old fossils the size of small buildings. Along with the dinosaurs, my favorite place to be was the incredible rooms with the dioramas. The scenes depicting the Native Americans' lifestyles were hypnotic to me. I would press my nose up against the glass and actually feel like I was there in the scene.

I closed my eyes hard and grabbed my bag a bit more tightly, bringing myself back in the moment, also trying to enjoy and stay connected to those memories. I was back in this incredible place, overwhelmed by the feeling of the energy, life, history, and legacy of this great institution; now, I was here as an adult for a meeting about some very important issues.

Standing there in the entrance, I could see from the left that Dr. MacPhee was approaching. Tall with lustrous curly salt and pepper hair, a neatly trimmed gray beard, and a chiseled mouth, he had the confident walk of a seasoned adventurer. Smartly dressed in classic jeans, a white button-down, and tweed blazer, he approached and pointed at me. I'm pretty unmistakable with my long white-blonde hair running halfway down my back.

I am a firm believer in being true to who you are. If you feel good in your clothing, then you will feel confident and good about yourself.

My jeans, tall boots, and a smattering of native jewelry & belts are how I roll. Today was no different. Ross must have googled me, as he spotted me right away, and I, him.

He marched with a purpose calling out, "Manda?" I smiled and shook his hand. His palms felt like luffa pads, likely from long days at digs and playing with rocks and fossils.

"Dr. MacPhee," my face suddenly feeling flush like a schoolgirl meeting a longtime crush for the first time.

"Call me Ross," he smiled warmly and motioned for me to follow. "Come up to my office."

I felt like I was floating as I followed his march to the elevator. Meanwhile, he was wasting no time getting started.

"You know, I believe in the horse. The horse has gotten a raw deal, and I want to see better things for the horse in general," speaking authorially as he very purposefully pushed the up button.

Ross used his key card to launch us to the fifth floor. I couldn't even respond to anything as the doors opened to a brown and black patterned linoleum floor that must have been installed during the 50s or 60s. The walls of the narrow hallway were lined with huge glass cases containing skeletons on metal rods and stands; pieces, parts, and full bodies strewn about on either side.

"Wow," I gasped, taking a beat to stare before me.

"Cool, huh?" Ross stopped for a half a beat, too, but quickly continued down the hallway.

It was hard to make myself focus on what he was saying with all of the fascinating surroundings behind the scenes at the Museum of Natural History. I almost tripped as we walked past doors leading to offices, conference rooms, and science rooms. My boots caught on the vinyl as I peeked inside a lab where a woman in a white coat was mixing something in a beaker, smoke billowing out of its brim. In another office, two very important looking scientists were talking animatedly.

It was unbelievable to be back here in this revered institution that I'd grown up admiring. Ross was continuing to talk about something else related to horses that I was totally missing as I was taking everything in.

Neatly cluttered with books, instruments, and a few photos of Ross' exploits around the world, his office was large and dark. He grabbed the cord to open the wooden blinds and let in some light. I noticed that not much more came in. Ross's office opened to a window facing the backside of the museum.

A few small tables were strewn with books, yellow notepads filled with pen ink notations and fossils, and in the left corner, a large coat rack topped with a raincoat and a brown woolen coat. His chair wasn't behind his desk but rather to the side, so there was no barrier to our conversation.

Already I felt more engaged as I went to sit across from him, setting my bag down on an easy chair in the corner. I looked around to spot book titles such as End of the Megafauna—The Fate of the World's Hugest, Fiercest, and Strangest Animals, Endangered—Exploring the World at Risk, and The Rise of the Present-Day Mammals, all books by Ross MacPhee.

A legend for his work in tracking the extinction of mammals from North America over 11,000 years ago using ancient DNA, he's traveled to the far reaches of the planet to collect data, mostly in the form of fossils; sometimes big fossils. I looked over to see a photo I recognized from a Scientific American article of Ross somewhere north of Siberia alongside a mammoth tusk larger than his six-foot-tall body.

"So how can I help you?" Ross asked as he grabbed what looked like a totally black yellow notepad and flipped it to the back page. Realizing it was already full, he turned it over to write on the notepad's cardboard backing.

Without even waiting for me to start into it, he went into full lecture mode.

"There's no argument. Horses, as we know them today, absolutely arose in North America. But, the history of the family of Equidae goes very much further back, at least 50 million years. And what I'd also like to point out is that despite that very lengthy history, horses have never been absent from this continent, except for the period between 10,000 years ago and 500 years ago. They disappeared 10,000 years ago with a lot of other big mammals, a short blip really in history. Prior to that, within the last 1000 years, the lineage of the domestic horse Equus caballus got into Asia, from North America, over the land bridge that existed at that time between Eastern Asia and Alaska.

There they prospered, eventually getting down into Africa, throughout Europe, and so forth. Horses got domesticated at least once, maybe several times beginning 6000 years ago in Eurasia. That led to the domestication of the horse and man's desire to interbreed many different breeds. Are you following?" Ross asked.

"Yes," I replied right away. I was actually riveted but trying so hard to stay focused on comprehending what he was explaining to me. I was focusing so hard that I felt like my ears would start smoking.

Ross barely waited for me to finish my one-word answer.

"Good. It doesn't matter from an evolutionary point of view. If you make the argument that the lineage of Equus caballus arose in North America, then they had the misfortune to disappear for a while and then circled back 500 years later, then in effect, it's no story at all. The domesticated horses were part of the fauna. They were away for a while and returned. There's no other way to conceive of this. A horse is a horse, that kind of thing."

Ross looked like he was waiting for me to catch up. "Great," I said and nodded for him to go on.

"We're working on tracing relationships—in this case on the basis of genetics, from older samples, fossils—all the way up to the present time. We've been working on it for the last several years with Beth Shapiro, a quite renowned ancient DNA specialist whose lab is at the University of California, Santa Cruz. Using fossil samples, we see to what degree we can trace the nature of the relationship between modern horses, modern domestic horses, and horses that lived in the past."

As I listened to Ross speak, I was organizing in my mind how to explain what I was doing and hoping to impress him.

"This country was built on the back of a horse. We wouldn't be here unless for horses," I interjected, throwing up my hands. "How is it possible that this country considers horses an invasive species? The only reason is that it fits a political agenda. Horses are a global species; they built every civilization on this planet and adapted to every environment."

I could see he was listening to me, so I continued to list out all of the things I was working on, from the UN event to a film, to my legislation and relationship with Congressman Israel and his Institute of Politics. I tied in his native species argument to what might be potential legislation. He took that as his cue to continue.

"I know 10,000 years sounds like a long time, but it's really not. Generally speaking, that's not enough time for species divergence to take place. We still haven't found the exact piece from that time, but our scientific evidence on this is strong. It would be hard to discredit that they are native. But when we submit information and studies to Washington to the various bureaus, it goes straight into the garbage or gets buried among other things."

I'm sitting there thinking that this Ross MacPhee is my knight in shining armor. Here is a man with deep credibility and scientific knowledge. If he and Beth prove horses are a native species, then they get certain protections by law and land.

I did innately know that even though the evidence would be there, it is not what the BLM or the cattle lobby want to have happen, and they would fight tooth and nail to discredit those findings.

I could hear the frustration in Ross' voice, and I knew he was right and what he was up against. DC politics was all about easy answers.

He looked up to the clock and said, "I have someone coming to see me at 12 about a Sloth. It won't take too long. Can you wait? We should continue this conversation."

It was hard to imagine that an hour had already passed since we were chatting away. I had made some plans for the rest of the day but could certainly come back. I responded with, "Yes, but later."

Ross replied, "I think this is really important that we finish this conversation."

We agreed to reconvene at 3:00 p.m. I headed out into the city for a few other meetings and rushed back to the museum to, once again, be on time. The security guard remembered me from my Audrey bag and signaled for me to go on up, and I did. I was now a regular at the Museum of Natural History. Ross met me at the elevator, and back we went to his office to finish our talk.

Our earlier discussion had been mulling in my mind, so I got right to it, "So, how close are you, and what else do you need?" I had been thinking about a myriad of things since our first talk. I was curious because if Ross could pin down this evidence, we could present it to the politicians just as they like to receive things on an easy sheet of paper, and this one would have a seal from The American Museum of Natural History.

"We need to collect more data from other museum collections or even do more excavations in places like central parts of North America; I am particularly interested in Oregon for some reason. Maybe even in South America, to see whether we can document how closely, and for how long, these hybridization events occurred. If we can push it back, even more, maybe right up to the end of land bridge times, which would not have been until about 20,000 years ago, which is really yesterday; then the argument that North American horses were different from those of Eurasia is null and void."

Having had time to think about all this, I chimed in with, "Well, it's all very CSI. So, you're extracting molecules from DNA from these ancient horse bones and carbon dating?"

"Yes, you can take that DNA material, and using special techniques in the lab, extract information from it. That's the reality. One of the issues that we face is that we then take this hard-earned information, and we disseminate it in user-friendly ways in scientific journals and such; the government agencies are burying this information in back rooms."

"Depending on what agendas it serves or doesn't serve," I added, rolling my eyes, knowing this all too well. "Like information that shows that horses are not environmentally damaging. That they actually are helpful, not harmful to the grasslands."

"This would really be a war to fight in DC with the almighty cattle lobby and their congressional puppets," I thought to myself.

"Exactly. Horses are grassland animals. The way their incisors work, they actually help keep the lands healthy and contribute to biodiversity. They are much more beneficial and not destructive like cattle," Ross continued. "I was excited about the work but didn't see a way forward."

"I think we can work together to get the information to where it needs to be, to make people care. Listen, Ross, I've been at this for over a decade, and I've had a lot of pitfalls. I'm still finding the right team and the right allies to move things forward with the American public and in Washington. I mean, it's a coup that we got this language into the FY2020 Appropriations Bill."

I explained in detail how former Congressman Steve Israel had helped us get language on rewilding into the FY2020 Appropriations Bill and the length of time Steve and I had been working together. "It's a major win because it's the first time the word, rewilding, is used in any legislation," I relayed. "Because we were able to get that legislation written into the appropriations bill, there could be future legislation protecting other animals and other species by leveraging rewilding and novel ecosystem opportunities. Two little sentences hiding in the bottom that, hopefully, nobody will pay any attention to because it has no funding appropriated to it."

Ross was leery of the word 'rewilding,' as it had such a broad spectrum of uses. Science is very targeted and exact, and the way people were using the word was of concern to him.

I listened to his concerns; my response to him was that since rewilding is so new in this country, we can determine what exactly defines rewilding and what the work will mean here in this country. We were creating and designing our own definition based on the natural world and ecological systems here in North America.

He didn't respond right away, but I could see he was thinking about what I said. I didn't want to get bogged down in the rewilding issues, so I quickly segued to the topic of the UN event. I was hoping to sell him on a spot with my upcoming event at the United Nations, which I thought was a big deal.

"Well, I've done events there before, you know," he said. "If you're planning a spring event, I'm not sure you have enough lead time at this point."

"Not enough lead time for April?" I ask incredulously. It was November! I felt like the UN was a really prestigious thing, and Ross had this look on his face like I was asking him to speak at the local library.

He continued to ask questions, many of which I didn't yet have the answers. It was quite the process to host an event at the United Nations. We were hosting a UN co-sponsored event, which was a whole other level of bureaucracy. Congressman Israel's team submitted the concept language for our event over the summer. It was November, and though they'd said the room was secured, our concept language for the invites hadn't yet been approved.

I had so many roadblocks to overcome in trying to get the event together. I wanted Steve to ensure that certain legislators attend and speak. Having spent the last decade running in political circles trying to wrangle politicians myself, I had begun to understand how they worked.

If you called up a congressman's office and said, okay, I have an event on June 5th, and we'd like the Congressman to attend. Their staffer would tell you to call back May 29th to see if he'd be available. On the opposite spectrum, dealing with a museum Ph.D. meant getting on his schedule twelve months in advance at a minimum.

We talked most of the afternoon about horses, politics, our families, my life in the New York area, and his travels around the world and beyond. We'd covered it all, but there was so much more. It felt like we'd known each other forever. I could tell Ross felt that, too. Synergy for a reason.

I secretly knew we had a job to do, and we each filled a niche, a need to bolster the work that we were each doing to help the horses and, ultimately, our rewilding initiatives. That's why we were brought together, and our cooperative missions seem to fit like a hand in a glove.

He walked me to the elevator, and I knew this was the beginning of something big. It was like an unwritten understanding that we were supposed to do this; to work together to prove that the horse was a native species, and that was a new way forward. It was my job, but it was now our job.

By the elevator, I reached my hand out to shake his and thank him for his time. Instead, he leaned over and gave me a tight hug. It took me by surprise for a moment, but I understood. We were kindred spirits, like-minded people with the same passion for the horse. It is not often that you find and connect with people on that kind of energetic level. It fills your soul in a way, and it renews your faith in the possibility of success as you are no longer alone in your vision. I am no longer alone on my island!

I walked out to 77th street and headed over to Columbus to grab a good old-fashioned yellow taxicab, and back to Penn Station. As I sat in the cab, I replayed parts of our conversation over in my head; I felt like I was a teenager again. I had to get a handle on myself. I was floating around in some alternate state. "Did that really happen? Dr. MacPhee is interested in collaborating with my foundation and me." I didn't know what the outcome would be, but I had a hunch that I had just received the help and support that I had been manifesting for a really long time.

The next day I sent the conventional thank you email and invited Ross out to the farm for a visit. I always feel the farm is a good representation of my legitimacy and authenticity. A few weeks later, we continued our conversation about Cana, and I shared with him my aspirations and how we might align to help the wild horses.

The puzzle pieces would be finally coming together to change the perspective and understanding of who the wild horses are to us; To create the future of rewilding horses on lands for an environmental benefit and to re-create a safe place for horses. Since we are unable to stand by their comradery from the past, we need to see the benefit that our precious horses still offer us. Not only do they heal us physically—as is shown in all the therapeutic programs for people—but they can also heal the lands. Whew! The small vision I live with.

Now, the next step would be to get Ross and Steve together to meet, but first, Ross and I would have one more meeting in the city. I picked the meeting spot, Serendipity 3. It had personal meaning for me because I'd gone there so much as a child. They also had a frozen hot chocolate that's just to die for, and I knew Ross was a chocolate guy.

I, of course, made a reservation, and when I arrived five minutes early, Ross was already waiting for me under the hot pink Christmas tree above the outdoor entrance, lined with colorful pulsing lights. Especially fun during the holidays, Serendipity 3 explodes with decorations. We walked into the cozy interior where Tiffany lamps were strewn with pearls and glass balls. An Andy Warhol hung over the table where we set to dine not far from a crackling fireplace.

"We got Warhol's table," I smiled at Ross, who pulled out a chair for me.

"I've never been here," Ross' eyes slowly digested the scenery. "Are you sure about this?" he said, looking at me like a scientist in the midst of a questionable experiment.

"Of course! It's a treat." I shared my whole history since childhood with this iconic place. Ross and I ordered a frozen hot chocolate. It came in a glass bowl the size of a small fishbowl. The creamy frozen chocolate mixture was topped with a mound of whipped cream strewn with chocolate sprinkles. I felt like I was a teenager again. Ross and I both leaned into our respective bowls and gave a first slurp through the cream-colored paper straw, decorated with golden stars.

"Oh, my God. That's good." Ross closed his eyes and smiled. He looked thrilled.

"I told you," I winked at him back. It's the small pleasures in life that we cannot forget are necessary. It's what makes us human.

"So, I wanted to follow up on our first meeting," I started into business. "I want to know how Cana Foundation can help with your work in proving that the horse is a native species to North America, as that will help further our cause in Washington."

Ross had already dented the dense chocolate dessert and looked down to notice he was consuming it too quickly. He let out a funny laugh.

"So, Beth Shapiro and I are working on research to establish whether these prehistoric horse populations share certain unique genetic markers or so-called fingerprints with modern domestic horses. Sharing would imply that all could be a single species, Equus caballus, making an objective case for the argument that horses ought to be considered part of the native fauna of North America." He paused and fumbled into his briefcase for a document. "Alisa Vershinina, a graduate student in the Shapiro lab, is using ancient DNA techniques to investigate the evolutionary history of horses at the end of the Pleistocene and to establish how these ancient populations relate to modern ones. By establishing the degree of genetic similarity among these populations, she has already made a number of important discoveries that bear on the problem of continuity. The results will be fully documented in her dissertation and the peer-reviewed scientific papers that will appear over the summer. But we need more funding." He pulled out a sheet on the research and handed it to me.

I'm nothing if not good at hosting fundraisers. From my Citi-Field events to parties I hosted in Wellington, Florida, during the Winter Equestrian Festival. I'd held parties and salons on my farm, bringing in top politicos and influencers to help, too. I knew I could get the money for Ross' project, but in exchange, I wanted Cana to be a part of it.

"The Back-Home Project," Ross said.

"What?" I asked as Ross took a big sip of the frozen mixture and had a sudden look of pain as he moved his palm to his forehead.

"Too fast. Brain freeze. We could call it the Back-Home Project."

"I like it, bringing our native horses back home where they are originally from. I think I can help you with the funding. It's a good excuse for me to throw a party," I winked at Ross.

Ross explained to me that the key was Beringia, the place where East and West meet. Most of Beringia is now submerged beneath the shallow waters of the Bering Strait, but during the ice ages of the Pleistocene it was dry ground. This is because so much of the Earth's free water was locked up in the ice that sea levels sank as much as 400 feet. Both animals and plants extended their ranges by crossing the Bering Land Bridge, as it's called. Among the animals were the megafauna, the mammoths, bison, bears, and of course, horses. If you want to establish whether horse populations from both continents freely interacted by crossing multiple times back and forth, thereby facilitating interbreeding and population continuity, you need a dropdead tool. That tool, Ross argued, was genomics. Prehistoric horse populations must have shared certain unique genetic markers or "fingerprints" with modern domestic horses. If those shared markers were not only present but maintained for long intervals in these prehistoric populations, then there must be an explanation, which would be continued interbreeding across the land bridge. All of this would point toward these groups, living or extinct, being a single species, Equus caballus. Critically, such a finding would make an objective case for the argument that horses ought to be considered part of the native fauna of North America. Yes, they left, but only for a few thousand years. That does not change their citizenship!

In the summer, Ross put me in touch with Beth Shapiro, professor of paleogenomics at the University of California, Santa Cruz, and her advanced graduate student, Alisa Vershinina. The Shapiro lab was using ancient DNA techniques to investigate the evolutionary history of horses at the end of the Pleistocene and to establish how these ancient populations may relate to modern ones. Alisa had already made a number of important discoveries that bear on the problem of continuity. However, her work was already being supported by federal and donor grants, making Cana Foundation funding unnecessary. Alisa's results will be fully documented in her dissertation and upcoming peer-reviewed scientific papers that will appear shortly. The Shapiro lab has already announced that there is good evidence for repeated, bidirectional movements of Pleistocene horses across Beringia, mixing their blood lines to some degree and providing exactly the kind of continuity that would be expected if these horses formed a very widely dispersed series of populations, or "metapopulations" in Eurasia/North America. Watch for headlines!

In the spring, if travel is possible, our team will go to the Yukon and then out west to Indian country, following the trail of oral history and native culture in search of more clues that will prove that the horse is the native species that we know it is and entitled to the inherent protections that citizenship provides. We will look for the appropriate lands on which to rewild our precious horses. I can't wait to make this trip and tell you about all the things that happen on this next leg of this journey, but for now, you will have to wait to see what happens next.

"Manda. I am encouraged by all of this," Ross cupped his frozen hot chocolate bowl in his hands, and I lifted mine for a toast..

"To the future, and do spare the horses."

13. BORN TO REWILD

A prayer for the wild at heart
Kept in cages
I know how you long
To run wild and free
To feel your blood pumping
To hear your heart beating faster
Yet you can't
For you are locked inside a prison

~Tennessee Williams, Stairs to the Roof

The following prose was a gift given to me on August 17, 2020, seven months into the pandemic, by Darrell Marcus - Kills In Sight, from Rosebud Reservation, South Dakota. He is a direct descendant of the great Tashunka Witko, also known as Crazy Horse.

The prayers are in our journey. Just untap the stream of blessings. It's a thunderstorm with a rain of inspiration and power that can nourish the seed that can grow the dreams; she is the sunrise.

I have read it over and over again and have come to understand these wise and powerful words. The inspiration has been running down like rain in my journey, and none more so since I was sick in mid-March with what I now know was COVID-19.

On March 11th, the World Health Organization had already declared that this was a pandemic, but our nation still hadn't asked citizens to lock things down the way Asian nations and Italy had already done. Things seemed to be changing quickly. On March 13th, Trump declared the virus a national emergency. Close to me, in New Rochelle, the area had so many cases that it was a containment zone. What people didn't know or didn't want to recognize was that COVID-19 had already proliferated, including to my area of Long Island.

On Friday, March 13th, I called my daughter Sabrina and pressed her to pack and leave her apartment in the city and come home to Long Island. There were all kinds of rumors about the city closing down and that nobody would be allowed in or out due to the virus.

My daughter, Sabrina, had just landed herself an internship with a small startup music company in the new hipster area of Brooklyn. Music is her passion, and she is hell-bent on whatever she feels, much like her mama. She aspires to be in A&R (artist and repertoire); scouting and representing young hip hop artists. Mingling in small, crowded music clubs, she spent much of her time scouting talent and networking, not the best situation during the onset of a pandemic. I had to enlist Albert's help to give me that extra push to get her home.

My son Daniel came home from college a few days later. As a freshman, he had been recruited to play lacrosse for the number one Division II team in the country. At the onset of his season, the school had decided to send everyone home mid-semester, meaning he'd do virtual classes for the next few months during the lead into summer and with no lacrosse season. Like the rest of the world, we were now all bundled up safely at home; dogs, horses, goats, and people.

Early morning of Monday, March 16th, I woke up feeling like crap. I remember lying there just knowing I had a fever and thinking to myself, "I can't believe I am getting sick and in the middle of a pandemic." There wasn't the slightest thought on my part that I would have the virus.

I turned over and looked straight at Albert and said, "where is the thermometer?"

I could see the look of shock in his eyes as he fumbled around in the bathroom, emerging with a digital infant thermometer from 18 years ago. Ugh, I would have to find it myself. When I did find some sort of thermometer that worked, sure enough, it read 101. I had a fever. Taking the thermometer out of my mouth for the fifth time, I thought, "This can't be! I don't get sick! Sure, I get the usual sinus infection every year, but a Z-Pak usually straightens me right out. I never miss a beat."

I ran to my cell and was able to make an appointment at the local urgent care. I thought if I get there ASAP, it will be early enough that I'll miss the crowds. I thought if I could get a Z-Pak that everything would be fine. That thought kept melding in with "who gets sick in a pandemic, only me." Round and round, those two thoughts went.

Albert was in his bathroom doing his usual morning rituals as men do when they are preparing for the day. Routine is everything to Albert. Me, not so much. I like to go with the flow, as they liked to say in the 70s.

I kept shouting into the bathroom at him, trying to be heard over his electric razor. "You don't think I have the virus, do you? I mean, I am prone to sinus infections, and, for a week, I already had the same type of post-nasal drip and issues I usually have this time of the year." I usually didn't have a fever, so there was a seed of doubt.

He clicked off the razor. His response was that of a couple married for a very long time, "No, of course not, honey. You're fine. Just go get the antibiotic."

The buzz of the razor started again. I sat on the end of the bed, staring down at Elliot, my little chihuahua, miniature pinscher mix who was sitting in his bed. I said, "Well Elle." as I called him, because he was my little man, "If I am going to die from some strange disease, remember I'm leaving you in charge."

Albert yelled out from the bathroom, "Are you going? You better hurry up before it gets crowded."

Ugh, was this really happening?

I kept going over in my mind. I eat well, drink just a little, work out, take a ton of supplements, and generally try to be Zen as best I can, and I always try to stay connected to my inner knowing, my soul self. So, I don't have the virus. I couldn't!

Fifteen minutes later, I arrived at the urgent care, masked, gloved, and sanitizer in hand. Remember, I am Lois' daughter, and with all her germ phobias and fear of illness, I was trained just for this circumstance.

In charge, as I was, I explained to the doctor that I had a sinus infection and only needed a Z-Pak. He listened to my chest, and as it was clear, so concurred. He refused to even test me for COVID. I left with a script for Augmentin and Purelled my way home and back up to the bedroom.

As I was convinced that I didn't have the virus, the kids and Albert were all in the same mindset. Isn't denial a great thing? I hunkered down on the big yellow couch in my bedroom, snuggled up with the dogs. Leila, the only German Shorthaired Pointer we have now, was like an electric blanket keeping me warm when the chills came with the fever.

The next few days flew by in a slow but certain haze. I barely ate anything. I went from no fever to a fever hovering around 102, and I felt so tired when the fever came that I could barely even watch Netflix. I kept getting these weird chills up and down my back, down my arms, and on the tops of my legs. It almost felt like it was neurological. Meanwhile, the cases in New York were growing by the day, and California had become the first state to issue a stay-at-home order, which occurred on March 16.

Over the next several days, I popped my Augmentin and managed the amount of extra-strength Tylenol and Motrin I was taking, being the naturalist that I am. The night fever and weird chills continued. I knew I'd lost several pounds when on morning three of my illness, my sweatpants seemed a little loose. After five days on Augmentin, I still wasn't feeling any better.

I made an appointment and went back to Urgent Care, armed and ready with my Purell and alcohol wipes. This time, the scene was totally different. There were people in hazmat suits standing in the parking lot directing us. I had my gloves, mask, and wipes but wondered if that was that even enough? Oh my god, I'm going back into this place, and now it's a whole crazy thing.

This time, the doctor examined me with a mask and shield. Again, I was told that my chest was clear and that maybe I had a viral sinus infection. He said he didn't have any test kits left for COVID. Instead, he did a viral panel for the flu. This time, I went home with a prescription for a Z-Pak.

Two days into the Z-Pak and my stomach was done. I assumed it was from the antibiotics. Even when I finished the Z-Pak, I still had a fever every day at the same time. Between 12:30 and 1 pm, it would creep up on me. With the fever came horrible headaches. Everything felt so dark. I remember sitting up at three in the morning and just thinking that I felt like I was in a science fiction movie. It felt like something dark had taken over my body, and I had no control.

I'd stay up at night as late as I could, laying on the couch and then moving to the bed. I watched every single episode of Friends. I was binge-watching four different channels, but they all seemed to be playing Friends. It was such a happy show, mindless entertainment but harkening back to a better time. I was nostalgic for Friends; this is when I really knew I was ill.

At one point, seven days into the same rigorous fever routine every day, I had myself a good ol' cry. I thought I would never get better, and the fever would never leave. I was told that sinus infections could have a fever for up to fourteen days, so I thought it could be normal to have a fever this long with a sinus infection.

I worried during this time about so many things. What about the horses and the foundation? What if I didn't make it through. Who would save them? Aside from my dogs, which helped to get me through this crazy time, was Erin King-Sweeney.

Erin was the newly appointed executive director of Cana Foundation. We had met two years ago on the legislative panel at the Hampton Classic. She is Congressman Peter King's daughter and was a councilwoman on Long Island at the time. Steve is good friends with her father, and they love horses. She is beautiful and has the most wonderful way about her. She is practical, pragmatic, and a lawyer, but the thing I love most about Erin is her attitude about life. She is always happy and believes there should be no reason why people can't work together and get things done, no matter what side of the aisle they stand on.

We hit it off right away, and I reached out and invited her to the farm for lunch. Erin always shows up fashionable and charming to any meeting or event. That day was no exception. One thing led to another, and I asked Erin if she would help me with Cana. Over time, she'd become the executive director; I was honored that she accepted the position.

During the pandemic, I never let on to anyone how I was truly feeling and how ill I was. The pandemic was causing havoc in the world, and everyone was on lock down, but it was Erin that kept us going. She was thinking of ideas and organizing video conferences. I invented a mysterious camera issue with my computer as I didn't want anyone to see me the way I was. She kept the energy going while keeping us in the game. Because of Erin, we didn't miss a beat; we were creating our plan for the future. It's during COVID that the plan for our online Zoom conference with Steve's Institute of Politics at Cornell came about.

People are always shocked when they hear Erin is working with Cana. The first thing they say is, "Isn't she a Republican?"

My response to that was, "We are two women that care about horses & the environment and want to show the world how to get things done together. We are not defined by a political party, gender, or stereotype. We are good people getting things done, doing good things for the right reasons;" and so it goes.

Erin came on full time around the same time Ross came into the picture, and everything seemed to be going along better than I could have hoped, as long as I didn't die from some mystery ailment. That may have put a crimp in my plans.

I spent a lot of the time mentally envisioning myself healthy and working with energy to heal myself during my illness, all continued learning experiences for my own personal growth. I'd always had faith, so why should this time be any different. I believe that I am here for a purpose and a reason greater than myself, and I have to be here to fulfill my purpose. It is my job.

Eventually, I would get better. It would be sixteen days in total until my fever broke for good. That morning, I opened up the window and let the smell of wildflowers and grass come inside. You know when winter's finally ending, and you get those first beautiful days of spring, and everybody's running outside to enjoy it? Everything looked so green and warm that just by seeing the outside world, I did start to feel like things would get better. The newness of spring gave me hope, and I was better.

My home is my sanctuary, my rewilding space. I'd been on Long Island almost my whole life, growing up with a mix of nature and New York City, but it was nature that always called me back. Now, with the land at the farm, my dogs, horses, bees, blue jays, red robins, woodchucks, deer, foxes, and even most recently, goats, I was allowing nature to show me what she wanted to be and how she worked. Nature was re-creating herself in front of my very eyes through the various kinds of insects, birds, and animals that were appearing and all the many species of plants. It wasn't just that they were showing up; it was how and where you would find them. The way nature was weaving back together with her song upon the land at the farm.

While our neighbors spent a mint on landscaping, I'd spent money to have the landscapers not cut the grass. The noise of a lawnmower sent chills down my spine. Within grass that now grew three feet tall were all sorts of flowers and bugs, ecosystems in all their glory, my own little Areas of Restorative Kindness, or ARK.

Feeling as sick as I had it only reaffirmed the value and importance of open spaces and habitats to human health, both physically and mentally.

The way the grasses grew in the paddocks where the horses grazed and the way they moved around the animals that came into their paddocks to share their habitat was fascinating to watch. The way the birds and the bee's pollinated the farm and to see plants that were located all the way on the other side of the property—now growing in the most unlikely of places—was the way things were supposed to be.

There are no such things as weeds here. They are plants that have landed in the wrong places. I know that dandelions are considered weeds, but who decided that? I even have a sign that says dandelion farm.

My dandies in spring
are my favorite of things
How grandly, the dandi can sing…

Sometimes I just bust out in rhyme. It's a thing.

They are such a happy flower and so beautiful. They have powerful healing properties and do a lot to help the soil. They even fertilize the grass.

The wild of the farm has an energy that is different than anything else I have ever felt. You can feel its life, its beating heart, while at the same time, it is calming and soothing all around you. Being away from the farm for any length of time, I start to feel like something is missing inside of me. It is palpable. Coming home to this place feeds my soul. It does for anyone that visits. That is what nature does for us if we allow her to connect us to our true selves. As nature flourishes, so do we. This is critical to understand at any level, whether you live in nature or in a city.

I was grateful that I had this place to recuperate. I was able to draw from nature to help strengthen and rebuild myself. Breathing wasn't an issue for me, so, based on that, it was just a matter of building myself back up; mentally and physically. The plants and the horses, even the goats, played a role in helping me to heal. Everything on my farm just made me feel alive and connected, an amazing feeling. It reminded me why I do what I do and profoundly reaffirmed why the horses need us.

The months in lockdown trickled by. I was busy organizing the care of the horses and the farm, feeding the family, and getting food and supplies while handling everyone's emotions. It was a lot, but I managed to keep the Cana work current and plan the next steps. We continued to work on the native issue of the horse and environmental study with Ross. Erin's networking and planning were squeezed in somewhere each day. We women can do anything if we put our minds to it.

Mo sometimes talked about the role of women in tribal communities and how their strength is felt and used by the whole community. Women bring life, run their households, serve on councils, and act as leaders. The great warrior chief Sitting Bull used to take council with thirteen women. Perhaps we've gotten traits passed down from these amazing souls.

It wasn't until June that I was able to take an antibody test. It confirmed what we all had thought. I had COVID antibodies, and so did Albert and the kids. I was one of the lucky ones. I got away relatively unscathed, but so many Americans and people around the world have been infected and died. COVID-19 has caused world hunger and economic depressions globally, and why? Why did this happen?

After I got past the anger of it all, I was able to see what needed to be done and how to take the situation and turn something horrible into something that would be of greater value for the future. There was an opportunity to point out why environmental sustainability and our horses are so critically important. This horrible pandemic and the illness it has brought doesn't ever have to happen again. Hundreds of thousands of people that have lost their lives and families who have been affected by this would not all have been in vain if we use this to demonstrate how and why we are so out of balance.

We had the rare chance to change what we had done wrong, to think about the future, our children, the planet, future generations of all inhabitants, including four-legged and two-legged species. I hoped that the pandemic would give us the light to allow us to work together and unite for something greater than ourselves. The horses could help to bring healing to the people and the planet, for our future.

Through the lens of indigenous teachings, the pandemic shows us one thing. It shows us that if we don't work together, like a colony of bees or a herd of horses, we won't survive. We all have to wear masks now. We all have to be mindful. We all have to be considerate of each other because we all share one home, one planet, and one place. If we don't think about others and the greater good and the future, we won't have one. Diseases like COVID-19 point this out to us in horrific and brutal ways.

In speaking to Mo over the phone through this, I understood exactly as did he.

"You know, I've seen it," he said. "And the next one that's coming is going to be worse. If the people think this is bad, wait until they see what's coming next."

And that is true. That is the fear. If we don't learn from this, what happens next will be worse.

I knew that at this point, if we didn't take action, we'd end up living these sheltered, frightened lives like we were now, in quarantine. We need to change our outlook and our understanding of our connection to nature and the environment, but all of our resources will be running toward medical research and science-based cures instead of going back to the root of the problem. Through our science-based information, we can show the importance of our horses environmentally and why they help us preserve open spaces for environmental health and sustainability.

Even amid the pandemic, the government was still planning on massive roundups of 50,000 horses and continued destruction of our public lands for special interest groups. Following this news only served to drive us further and faster with our foundation and research plans.

My wheels have been churning and burning with these thoughts and ideas. You cannot go forward if you don't understand the past. We must rebuild the environment with the help of our large mammals, or megafauna, as my friend Ross refers to them, but this time with a greater connection to understanding and respecting our relationship to all living things.

Manmade chemicals and pesticides are killing everything, including us. Did you know that scientists have found that the number of birds in the United States and Canada has declined by three billion, or twenty-nine percent, over the past half-century? This is mostly due to chemicals and climate change. I read that there is a 43 chromosome difference between wheat and what companies like Monsanto have done to the wheat that we eat. There is only one chromosome difference between monkeys and people, so you can imagine what the wheat would look like if it were a person.

A report put out by the United Nations in May 2019 states:

"Ecosystems, species, wild populations, local varieties, and breeds of domesticated plants & animals are shrinking, deteriorating, or vanishing. The essential, interconnected web of life on Earth is getting smaller and increasingly frayed. This loss is a direct result of human activity and constitutes a direct threat to human well-being in all regions of the world."

~Professor Settele.

The report also states that around 1 million animal and plant species are now threatened with extinction, many within decades. This is more than ever before in human history.

These are crisis-level statistics when you think about the future and what we have all just experienced through the pandemic. But here's the good news, as the native spirits say, "It is the beginning of many new sunrises."

Each day brings a new beginning and a new opportunity to try harder and be better. The world is for our enjoyment to share in all the beauty that is here for us. We just have to remember who we are, find ourselves, and we will know how to live happier and more fulfilled lives. Lives that have balance, without inequality, hatred, and with compassion and reason. These are the things that my horses and my journey have taught me.

As I look back on the journey that my horses have taken me on for the last thirteen years, I reflect on my many mistakes and poor choices. Believe me; there were many. There were many times that I wanted to quit and actually declared that I was finished chasing this unobtainable dream. It would only be a day or two later that I would find myself planning and plotting what needed to be done and how I would do it. But there were also many wonderful people. Relationships I have forged and adventures I have had. These all have been my life lessons, and I welcome their teachings.

Although horses are just one cog in a greater wheel of life, they need our help, and they have been the one thing that has been the constant in man's history. The history of man is the history of the horse. Taking the issues on is something that I can do to help, and so can others, because saving our wild horses saves the environment and shows the need for rebuilding our relationships with nature and the planet we call home. This can only result in positivity and good. To save the people, we have to save the horses, and to save the horses, we have to save the people. It is synonymous, recursive, and perfect.

So here we are, at the end of this little literary journey. When I set out to write about my experiences, I was concerned that with all the other memoirs and books from decision-makers and influencers in the world, why would anyone want to read about me? Why should what I have to say matter? Then I realized that the answer is simple; it all matters, and we are all a part of the same story. I am no different than you. We are all the same, and if I can learn and walk this path, so can we all.

At the beginning of my story, I was lost; on a quest to find myself. You might be wondering, "Am I any more found today than I was when I started my journey?" Well, that depends on what found looks like. There is no doubt I am much more connected and much more in tune with who I am, my strengths, my weaknesses, my flaws, and my failures. Knowing all these things is only good if you stand in the truth of what they are and acknowledge the things that are good. Acknowledging the things that could be better helps me know where I am and navigate my path forward.

I know that I have a destined path, and I know what that path is; for that, I am grateful. Understanding what needs to be done is half the job. Everybody does different things. Everybody has different opportunities. You don't have to run out and save wild horses. Maybe your journey here is simply to be happy, just to find and connect to what makes you happy and to be true to yourself. I don't know. You have to figure that out.

But what I do know is that we all have gifts and talents that are unknown to us. We all have the ability to do whatever we choose and be whoever we choose. Believing in ourselves is the hardest part. I know because I question myself every day, but if the universe believes in me, who am I to argue?

I am now preparing my next leg in my quest to save America's wild horses. I'll be working from home like everyone else for the foreseeable future. I'll organize video conferences with interested people, and I'll share what we learn.

I am setting my mind to working on orchestrating the use of the rewilding language from the Appropriations Bill. Going forward in 2021, this will enable us to marry environmental rewilding with wild horses and green energy. There are giant environmental opportunities, as well as socio-economic, and not just for native communities, but for our public lands as well as private. It's my best lesson yet.

Then, for Ross to prove that horses are a native species, we need to find this missing artifact from over 13,000 years ago, when the horses disappeared. That missing artifact is on American Indian lands. It's from our native peoples. I know this, and I know where we have to start.

I feel strongly that the piece of bone is woven together in some coveted ceremonial tool held by a spiritual leader. They probably don't even know what's inside. It's just been passed down and passed down, but it's in there. We have to find it.

In the spring, our team will go to the Yukon and then out west to Indian country, following the trail of oral history and native culture in search of a missing artifact that will prove, conclusively, that the horse is the native species to North America that we know it is and, as such, is entitled to certain protections. We will look for the appropriate lands to rewild our precious horses on.

I will continue to "Untap the stream of blessings in a thunderstorm with a rain of inspiration and power that can nourish the seed that can grow the dreams. She is the sunrise."

Native lore speaks about following the trail of history to find modern answers. We need to change our outlook and our understanding of our connection to nature and the environment.

Without our connection to our planet, we are forever and truly lost.

14. WHAT NOW?

Imagine my excitement when, late in October, shortly after submitting this manuscript to my publisher, I received an email from Ross. It was somewhat cryptic, saying only, "Manda, we have to talk!" "Uh-Oh," I thought, silently panicking. "I wonder what's going on; that's not like him to be so vague." Although Ross does not conform to the usual stereotype of the scientist, he can be very serious about things from time to time. This was feeling like one of those times. I rushed to email him right back; unnerved by his tone but also curious.

"Ready to chat when you are," I replied. Ross' reply was immediate.

"Let's set up a video call; it will be easier for me to explain."

Now I was really curious.

We agreed to speak the next morning; I had all night to let my imagination run away with me. My mind darted between Ross quitting the project to Ross finding the missing fossil evidence, to all sorts of anxiety-induced scenarios. By the time the morning came and I got on our call, I was exhausted!

"Good morning, ok, I am ready; what's going on?" What Ross was about to tell me, if not mind blowing, was certainly attitude-altering; for him, that is. Ross began.

"I was not going to tell you this right away, I wanted to wait to be sure because I knew you would be hysterical."

Now I was hysterical, silently anyway. He continued.

"Manda, you have to keep this confidential for the time being, but a grad student of Hendrik Poinar, my long-time collaborator, has just made an incredible discovery. The student's name is Tyler Murchie. He has genetic evidence for the presence of horse DNA found in sediments only 5800 years old. He has just had his preliminary paper on his findings accepted by *Quaternary Research*, a well-respected science journal."

Now one moment, let's recap. As part of the effort to show that the horse should be regarded as a North American native species, we need fossil evidence optimally, evidence indicating that the horse might have survived here long after 10,000 BC, the end of the period of the great extinctions when most large mammals—or 'megafauna,' as they are called—disappeared on this continent.

As you now know, I believe that Native American oral traditions are inspired statements akin to revelations. While they may not be up-and-down factual, they often parabolically speak to greater truths. You just have to know how to listen to them. They are the backbone of native traditions and customs. Native lore had always spoken of the horse being here long before the Spanish arrived. There are stories of native people living in caves underground with their horses, along with petroglyphs of horses displaying specific markings representing, among other things, various periods of time.

Ross, being a man of science and facts, has always said to me, "There just isn't any hard evidence for the continued presence of horses in North America after the megafaunal extinctions. I have to go with the facts as they are, not what I'd like them to be. It would be fantastic if we had verifiable Holocene-age horse fossils. We would absolutely mine them for genetic material. But there aren't any. All the supposed examples I have heard about just scream 'bogus' to me."

Although I respected Ross' position, me being who and how I am, I just knew that there had to be some form of fossil evidence to stand by the native history, which speaks of small pockets of horses surviving through the post-extinction period. These oral traditions just had that ring of 'greater truth.' So, we basically agreed to disagree about 'Holocene horses.' Although, I have always told him that I would prove him wrong and find the missing evidence for him.

But, back in the present, Ross continued: "Now, Manda, 5800 years ago sounds like a lot, but this discovery puts the history of the horse in North America in a wholly different light: survival!

"Ross, hold your horses! Are you saying that there is a smoking gun and that there is DNA evidence in dirt sediment proving that horses were here during the Holocene period?

I was so excited I could hardly breathe; I knew it. Deep down, I just knew it!

"Well," Ross said, sounding cautiously optimistic. "Although the signal on the readings is a little weak, I have thought about all the possible arguments against this interpretation, and I am convinced that yes, this evidence does speak to horses being here during the Holocene period."

I sat speechless for a moment, which is quite something for me. Then, with a sassy smirk, I said, "So, you know what this means, don't you?" I could see Ross smiling, "Yes, Manda, you 'might' be right about the Native Lore and oral history regarding the horse."

"Well then," I said resolvedly, "we better get past this pandemic so we can go out west and look for that fossil I owe you."

"Yes, I am all in. Now, let me explain how Tyler and Hendrik found the DNA; it's actually quite amazing.

They took cores in various special places in Siberia and eastern Beringia. They purposely looked for contexts that were likely to include very recent, undisturbed fine sediments—the kind of dirt in which tiny bits of isolated DNA might attach to certain minerals like quartz. DNA that occurs in this way is called environmental DNA because it is not attached to anything like a recognizable fossil, like a bone or plant part. As crazy as it sounds, such nanosamples of DNA can be studied and give an answer to the question, "Whose DNA is this anyway?" Using special software, the genetic sequences on these tiny fragments can be read and compared to thousands of complete genomes in huge databases. If the recovered DNA has known species-specific markers, then this information can potentially be used as a kind of barcode.

Ross concluded, "It can tell you if species X was present at a specific level in a core. If there is datable material at the same level, like bits of charcoal that can be dated by radiocarbon, then not only do you get the species, you get the timeframe it was living in."

That is the kind of unbelievable twofer that made Ross dance a jig (viewer discretion advised; not recommended for family viewing).

That may sound kind of easy, but it isn't. First, you can have DNA from innumerable sources in a cubic centimeter of a given core. In the analysis, you have no control beyond being able to grab whatever DNA is in the sample and synthesize enough of it to study. Unsurprisingly, this is called "shotgun amplification." But thanks to the aforementioned software, it is possible to determine if any target organisms are present with reasonable efficacy.

Do that with enough different sequences, and you get a biological snapshot of the kind of diversity that existed. Tyler found horse and mammoth, as well as many other creatures that are still with us. Not just once, but numerous times in cores from several different sites in the Klondike region of Yukon. These could be time-stamped using various dating techniques, right up to the most recent radiocarbon date, right in the middle of the Holocene, 5800 years ago. Because Tyler was primarily interested in trying to reconstruct past ecosystems, he set about identifying the dozens of species of plants and animals represented in the DNA, all of which he carefully documented to build the picture. So not only do we know that horses and mammoths were still present in northwestern North America when the ancient Near East was just entering the Bronze Age, but we can also reconstruct the environments in which they lived.

Ross, being Ross, naturally wants more. Working with Tyler, Hendrik, and other colleagues, he wants to expand the environmental DNA study to other areas in northern Canada and Alaska. Although horses may well have survived in other parts of North America, the far north is the place to look initially because it has been persistently cold for a long time, which helps to preserve DNA. To this end, the team will conduct new research with the support of the Cana Foundation. Tyler's follow-up paper, in which his results will be presented in full detail, is now being written up and should be available in 2021.

Now, what does all of this really mean in light of my journey? It is what I have always believed: the greater truth, embedded in the stories of Native Americans, is there to be found by those with the eyes to see.

So, to wrap it up, what can I say? You and I have things to do!

Scan the code to get in the mood for what's next.

With love, Manda

And hey, if ya wanna save some horses,
and the world—reach out, won't you!

THE END
And yet, we begin

Scan this code to see the full
www.BornTotewild.com/gallery

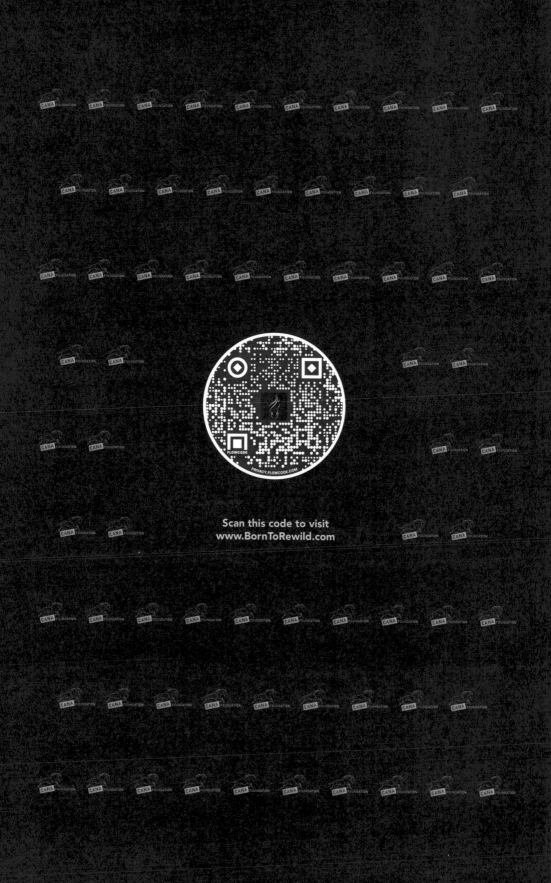

Scan this code to visit
www.BornToReWild.com